Recapturing Fate

ISBN-13:9798338802106

Dedication

To… My past, my present that's
leading to my beautiful future.
People who are
meant to be together will always
find their way back to each other.
They might take
detours in life but they are never
lost.

Chapter 1

This was where it started; the pain was sometimes unbearable. There was the joy of being with those certain people, only to be hurt by them in the end. The ones she loved became lost at some point. The anxiety of thinking… how would things turn out for her? She didn't want to turn out like the people she assumed loved her.

Her parents were divorced before she left, they were so miserable with their lives that they didn't even acknowledge her existence. Her whole life she tried to accomplish the hardest things to gain just a bit of attention. That's where everything started. Her family… her family what could she say they only consisted of her and the people who gave her a life and then basically ignored her. No siblings for her when she needed them the most.

Honestly, they didn't deserve the title of parents. They still didn't. All twenty-six years of her life were based on what she did wrong and what caused her 'family' to end up how they were. She listened to their conversations they went from whispers to shouting in seconds. If they couldn't bear each other, why hadn't they just divorced while she was at an early age? She would have rather been tossed between them than stand in on the daily fighting matches. If that was their way of showing their love, they were terrible at it.

She stared out at the city where she had spent most of her life. She spent years in one city and then the next, but this one was where she learned how to live. This was where she understood the difference between people who lied and honest people. The difference between actual love and lust and that lust is easily given. That's why she moved from here when she had a chance. The melancholy feeling of this town had changed her perception of the world she wanted to see through her eyes.

She was overall a happy person. This place though changed her. She wasn't depressed or anything that made her seem dejected. She was just ultimately calculating. She parked her car on the mountain and looked out over this place. Her first feelings of love were sparked here. It was the kind of love a person would normally be envious of. It hadn't lasted as long as her heart hoped for, but she can say it wasn't that fake love she had come to know so well. It was real. That was eleven years ago.

She didn't know what happened to him. She didn't know if she missed him or not. In her mind, she had no clue why she had come back. She was already living that successful life she had only dreamed of so long ago, only now it was reality. She sat in her car gripping the wheel while her thoughts of why she had been there plagued her. Why did she come back here?

All that she left in this town was complications and memories that she meant to leave in the past. She left this place quicker than she wanted to. After high school, there was no reason to stay. Even though she would have missed those people, she had set her mind on leaving before she knew if she'd graduate. She could have dropped out or something along those lines, but she stayed. Her memories had flooded back as she sat there. The cold, dreary weather she had become so accustomed to then, had turned a normal day into a freezing wreck.

She spent her day with her friends. The wind blew the light snow around and the feel of running on the cold ground prevented her feet from wanting to move anymore. Oh, how she craved for that memory to be re-experienced. For once she missed that unsympathetic weather. Where she lived now it was so warm and pleasant but when her mood drowned, she had wanted that weather to accompany it. While her memories pulled her into a trance, her phone rang. It was her mother.

She hesitated but answered. Since her mom had not been nice well, she could produce better words but being nice to her didn't mean she had to treat her the same way.

"What?" she answered in that harsh tone she had become used to using.

"That's no way to talk to your mother." Her mom had said in her annoying cheerful voice.

"And when have you ever been a mother to me?" she replied with so much venom.

"Oh sweetheart, don't say I never acted like a mother to you. I fed you and made sure you were alive. I also made sure you went to a good school and had good clothes. That's all that you needed."

Her so-called "mother" scoffed. Tears threatened to spill from her closed eyes. How could she say that she was a mother? This was why she left. Lies like that had made her disgusted.

Wasn't love an option in her mother's terms? "Don't lie to yourself. If you thought, you were a real mother you are delusional." She seethed into the phone.

"Is this because your father and I divorced?" her mother questioned curiously. She sighed. She didn't want to deal with this. Her mother didn't have a clue. She was so convinced she was a great mom, that it was hard to pull her out of schizophrenic daze.

"No, it's not. Look I'll pass by later. Bye." she said about to hit the end button.

"You're here? Back in this town! I thought you dashed out of here without planning to come back." Her mother laughed humorlessly.

"I did but I guess there's some unfinished business I have to deal with," she said before hanging up.

Chapter 2

Her life was so dramatic. That little phone call had turned her life around. In ten years, her mom hadn't talked to her and now that she was in her hometown, she called. Her mom hadn't even known she was coming here. Contemplating all this she started to drive away. Before fully leaving she turned her head to the view of the city lights. "A joy seeing you again old friend," she shouted into the wind. She drove away, not bothering to look back at what she left behind.

She drove back down the path and maneuvered her car back to the main street. She was wondering where her dad was. He hadn't talked to her either since she left. She shook those thoughts away and blasted her radio she needed to focus on something else. She started singing like a crazy person while looking around to see what had changed in her small town. Nothing changed. Before she went to her mom's house she decided to stop at the local diner. She had gone there all the time when she was a teenager. As she stepped out of her car she stalled for a minute, staring at the little diner.

Nothing changed with the fifties' design. She took her time walking to the door and entered the memory-filled warmth. As she entered everyone's eyes turned towards her.

"Well, I'll be darned if it isn't little Miss Aurora Mathews. Who knew you would show up in this place again? I heard you were hitting the big money down in Miami. You're a Chef now huh?" a server in her late sixties said walking up to her.

At first, she hadn't known who the server was but glanced at her name tag, which sparked remembrance. "Good to see you, Joyce." She smiled kindly to her old friend.

"You look great. Even better than I thought you would. It doesn't even seem like you were the ugly duckling in that group of yours. If you had stayed here, you might've won the hearts of all those boys you were crushing on in high school. Nobody but you and Tristan Alvarez left this place. You're here in time for the reunion. All of them are going to be at the high school gym tomorrow at twelve. Even Tristan since he's home for the holidays. It's not that surprising he's here though he comes home once a month. You, on the other hand, haven't been here in ten years. Did they tell you about that reunion?" she said so enthusiastically.

Aurora sat down at a booth she had remembered so well. "No, they didn't mention it. Looks like I'm going to be a surprise." She replied brightly.

Oh, how she loved high school. She never had problems with the people around her. They treated her with respect and made her happy. It annoyed her a bit that they hadn't told her about the reunion. She wondered if she had done anything in the past to cause them to want to forget about her. Truthfully, she decided to forget about this place so why wouldn't they?

"Do you want your usual?" Joyce said, breaking Aurora's thoughts.

"You still remember what I had?" Aurora said stunned.

"You're my favorite youngster. How could I forget you? I remember when you and that group of kids would come here." She smiled while writing on her pad of paper.

Aurora looked up at her and smiled. "That's good to know ma'am," Aurora said sweetly. Joyce smiled at her and walked away towards the kitchen. She sat and looked out the window. The rain had stopped a bit, but she knew it would come back within minutes. She heard her phone ring silently in her bag and positioned to answer it.

"AURORA! Where have you been? I've been looking for you everywhere. Your house, the apartment… your office? I even checked Mike's house just in case. I know you guys are over, but I had to check." Renee Hicks shouted into the phone.

Renee was Aurora's secretary and closest friend. Renee had that perfect family life Aurora only dreamed about. She wasn't jealous of Renee, but she sometimes wished she had her life.

"I'm not there Renee. I'm not going to be back three weeks." Aurora sighed into the phone.

"Where are you then? You have clients on hold and your boss is wondering where you are! You didn't tell anyone that you were leaving. Not even me!" Renee whined.

Aurora laughed slightly and responded, "I know Renee. I can't tell you where I am. It's a secret. I promise I'm not hurting myself in any way. It's more like a trip down memory lane." Aurora said giving a hint without meaning to.

"You're in your HOMETOWN!!" Renee screamed into the phone.

Aurora laughed loudly and replied between labored breaths, "Yeah I am." Renee told her she would be there in two days, but Aurora reasoned otherwise.

"No, you shouldn't. I'll bring you here some other time. Right now, I just need to stay here and figure things out." Aurora sighed yet again.

"Alright, you better not get in trouble there," Renee said before hanging up.

As Aurora hung up Joyce came back with her eggs and Taylor ham. She thanked her and was left alone again to ponder about what had happened while she was gone. When she finished Joyce came back around to ask if she needed anything else.

"No, I'm good. Take a seat here I got to ask you about what's been happening in this place." Aurora said while showing Joyce to a seat. Joyce sat and looked at her sheepishly.

"What's there to say? Your life must be more exciting than how things are around here. It's the same old city secrets and drama. You skipped out here quicker than I thought you would. Your parents were that bad?" she asked.

"Yeah, they were," Aurora said gloomily.

Joyce reached out to hold Aurora's hand. "I'm sorry dearie. I doubt they were ready to even have a family." Joyce said sympathetically.

"Yeah, it's all right. Nothing will change. Do you know where my parents live?" Aurora asked.

"Your mother still lives in your old house and your father moved into a new apartment," Joyce said calmly.

"Dad was the one who bought the house. Did he just give it to Mom?" she asked, shocked.

"Looks like it. I guess he just wanted to end it there without more problems." Joyce said while shaking her head. Aurora snorted.

"That's so like dad… Just… give up. I'm serious why did they have to raise me at such an early age? They were kids themselves when they had me. "Aurora said heatedly.

"I know dear. I'm sorry it turned out that way. Look why don't you go talk to your mom? You're here anyway." Joyce said calmly.

"I plan to… I'm just thinking about what to say. I tend to go straight to the point you know? I guess that's why I have the best kitchen in Miami." Aurora said with a smile.

Joyce blinked and smiled. After a couple of minutes, Aurora left the diner and walked toward her car. She entered her car and became nervous. "Breathe Aurora you got this." She chanted softly to herself. She drove off with more confidence than she ever had.

Chapter 3

As she pulled up to her old house, she felt tears threaten to fall yet again. She remembered playing in the front yard. Her parents were rich, and a lot of people thought she had the best life ever. If only they only knew. She would have rather had that middle-class life most people in her life had but they were rich. Money tore them apart. She had seen that happen a lot beyond her own family life.

Most ex-couples fought because of money. In her life, she revolved around those fights and pain that she sometimes wanted to shout at exes for not thinking about their children. The poor kids sometimes didn't know what was happening. It was heartbreaking. She pulled herself back to reality and started walking toward the door. Before she was fully at the door it opened. Maria Warner came out the door to greet her only child.

"Hello, Aurora." she said coolly.

Aurora looked at her mom who looked as she did ten years ago. At forty-six, she would have passed as Aurora's sister any day. That Brown hair they didn't share was immaculately tied into a ponytail. Her brown eyes had a glitter of hope in them but quickly disappeared after seeing her daughter's unhappy expression.

"Hello, Mom," Aurora said halfheartedly.

Maria motioned into the house and Aurora walked in shivering slightly. Those memories flashed back to her mind, but she pushed them down with fear of becoming vulnerable. Her mom hadn't even bothered to re-decorate the house they, as a family had decorated. Strange I figured she would. Maria walked in front of her and showed her to the kitchen.

They sat in silence for the first few minutes before her mom broke the silence.

"What brings you back to Woodland Park?" Maria whispered while playing around with her hands to distract herself.

"I wanted to see old faces. The city gets stuffy sometimes." Aurora said monotonously.

"Oh well, that's nice," Maria replied agitated.

The air between them became hostile. Aurora had enough. It was time to say what needed to be said.

"Look Mom here's the thing. I came back because I wanted to see you and Dad. I want a relationship with both of you since I never had one when I was younger. I want you all to be proud of me and understand that all I ever wanted when I was little was for you both to be active parents. I wanted you all to stop fighting. I wished we could have been a family. I would have rather you all divorced when you started having problems and be thrown from you to him. But instead of that you both shut me out of your life like I was the cause of this mess. You all never said I love you to each other or me for that matter. Didn't you ever think I was hurt by that? Did you ever think I wanted to be loved? Do you even care about me?" Aurora cried, pouring out all she had in her.

Maria was in tears. She didn't know this was how Aurora had felt all her life. Guilt spread across her and she cried. When Maria gave birth to Aurora, it was one of the happiest days of her life. She had a baby girl that was made with love between her and John, the love of her life. She hadn't known why their relationship had crumbled. One minute they were so much in love then the next they hated each other for so many reasons. She hadn't known she was secluding her little girl from that love that evaded herself. Aurora watched as her mother cried her heart out. It pained her to see her as such so she stood up and hugged her mom.

"I do love you, sweetie. I was so happy when I gave birth to you. Your dad and I had been looking forward to having kids and being a family, but things didn't turn out the way we wanted them to. Your father and I started to have problems and then it was irreparable. He was the love of my life and then in a flash, he was gone. I'm so sorry. "Maria bawled into her daughter's shoulder.

Aurora shushed her mom calmly and finally understood why she treated her how she had. It was all because of love. Her only love had shut her out and so she had done the same to the people she loved too. Aurora understood that feeling. Tristan Alvarez was her first love and the only one she had loved so strongly. He broke her very soul. They were about to have their fourth anniversary; everything was set up weeks before but on that awaited night Aurora was left at the restaurant table without a date. That ended it. She tried talking to him about why and his only excuse was because he had forgotten, and he had been busy with his friends. Her heart wouldn't stop breaking over and over again as she thought of that moment.

After that, she had dated so many guys, but the closeness was never there anymore. It was only he who struck that feeling in her. She wanted to feel that again. They hadn't even said goodbye to each other. Aurora sighed. She would see him tomorrow even if she didn't want to. She had to show all of them, she was still there, and she was always there.

"Look Mom it's okay. Don't cry." She said pained.

Her mom sniffled and wiped her tears away as Aurora sat down again.

"I'm sorry. I'm a mess." Her mother spluttered while laughing slightly.

They spent more than an hour talking. As the time dragged on Aurora asked where her dad was.

"He lives at this address, and he might be really surprised to see you. I'm not kidding; you looked like me when I was your age. Except for the eyes, you have your dad's eyes; so blue and luminescent." Maria said happily while passing her the new address of her dad.

Aurora stood up and headed towards the door. Before she exited the door her mom stopped her.

"Do you have somewhere to stay?" her mom questioned. Aurora turned around to face her.

"Actually, no I don't," Aurora said.

"Well do you want to stay here?" she asked through the pouring rain.

Aurora smiled and nodded. She got into her car and headed off to her dad's house. She walked slowly along the path and waited before knocking on his door. She heard a small noise behind the door and finally, a little girl answered the door.

Chapter 4

Aurora was shocked. Did her dad have another family?

"Who are you?" the girl questioned through her awestruck expression.

"Uh, I'm here to see John Mathews. Does he live here?" Aurora said shakily.

The girls' eyes lit up and quickly pulled Aurora into the house. She heard laughter and glasses clinking in the room. As they entered the room, she saw her dad and a remarkably familiar woman drinking in front of the TV. They turned their heads in her direction and her dad dropped his drink onto the carpet. He stood up and walked to her slowly.

"Aurora? Is that you?" he whispered as the woman on the couch stared shell-shocked. "Uh hi, Dad?" Aurora said uncertainly.

"It is you!!" her dad said while hugging her. He backed up and looked at her again. "Wow, you look just like your mother." He said with a smile. How could they have divorced if they seemed to love each other so much? They fought so much before but now as she was before her dad, he seemed to have that faraway look after he took sight of her.

Thinking of her mom…hum… "Thanks. Who's this?" Aurora said pointing to the little girl. "Oh, this is Dawn. She's your cousin." He said while hoisting the little girl into his arms.

Her heart seemed to stop as she viewed this sight. Her dad never carried her like this. She pulled all the negative thoughts away and smiled.

"Hi, Dawn. I'm Aurora." She smiled sweetly.

Dawn's eyes widened and she started wriggling in John's arms. He let her down and went to the woman on the couch.

"Mommy! Is that Uncle John's daughter? She's so pretty." Dawn asked in a whisper.

"Yes, it is. Doesn't she look like Aunty Maria?" Dawn's mom said in a whisper.

Dawn stared at Aurora with her big hazel eyes and nodded furiously. Her mom laughed at Dawn's display. Aurora turned to her dad and raised an eyebrow at the woman. The woman stood up and walked in front of Aurora.

"I'm guessing you don't remember me." The woman said while staring at her.

"I'm sorry. Who are you?" she said with an uncomfortable laugh.

"I'm your dad's sister. You're Aunt Victoria? I thought you would've remembered your favorite aunt." She said with a smile.

Truthfully, she did, just like she had forgotten Joyce, but after a minute recognition washed over her. Her Aunt Victoria had always given her big and glamorous gifts for her birthdays and Christmas. Aurora loved her for that.

"Of course, I remember you!" Aurora giggled while giving her aunt a small hug.

She didn't know how to approach her dad. Unlike her mom, her dad was a very unemotional man. He never cried or showed sympathy around her. It was mostly a faint smile or cold stare he gave out to others.

"So Aur why are you here? I'm glad to see you but why show up now? It's been ten years." Her dad said coolly.

"I wanted to talk to you and Mom," Aurora said.

Her dad looked at her questioningly. "About what?" he asked.

She hesitated a second before saying, "About how you and mom treated me when I was younger." Her dad was silent.

John didn't know how he treated his daughter. He regretted the fact that he never saw her that much. He had been so happy when Aurora was born. It was one of the happiest days of his life. She changed his life in an effective way. Maybe this was a part of her not seeing him that much, he thought painfully.

"How?" he asked curiously.

"Look Dad here's the thing. I came back because I wanted to see you and mom. My life is different because of how you treated me. Maybe if the two of you weren't so dysfunctional I would have been less mad at the world. God, I wished you would have stopped screaming at each other long enough to see the effect you had on me. You all had never even laughed together or anything! My friends had normal lives and parents who loved each other. You and mom only fought and acted like freaking children! You never did anything with me like normal dads. You all hadn't even gone to my graduation! What kind of parent does that? Why not… I don't know try to act like a dad!?" She shouted angrily.

He was acting like her mom had only an hour before. They both thought they were innocent. Her dad stared at her wide-eyed and with his mouth gaped open. John didn't know that this was how his angel felt. This was why she had left so quickly. Had she even said goodbye? Now he couldn't remember but his guilt would have lasted forever. He didn't cry but he felt as if she punctured a nerve. He didn't want to yell back at her by telling a lie that he was indeed a good father. He didn't entirely believe he was such a bad father, but he felt that he didn't do the best at his job.

Aurora had always been a strong girl. It showed through her personality and her piercing eyes. When she was little, she would stare at him and his wife as they fought. It pained them both that she had to watch such episodes, but they couldn't do anything about it. Maria always wanted her way, and he wanted his way. That's what went wrong. What made it more painful in the end was that John still loved her. Both of them were too stubborn. He knew he should have just listened to her, but he was stubborn. He knew Aurora had some stubbornness in her that came from them both.

"I'm sorry you had to go through that. I am." John said in a whisper.

Aurora's eyes flickered with aggravation. "Is that the best you got? Whatever." She snorted.

John frowned and raised his voice slightly. "What? Are you telling me I was a bad father?" he wailed.

Aurora walked toward Dawn and her aunt. "It was nice seeing you guys. I hope I'll see you around sometime." Aurora said with a genuine smile.

She started walking toward the door but stopped and glowered at her father. "No Dad, I'm not saying you're a bad father. I'm just saying you should have tried and fixed our family." Aurora said sarcastically.

She walked out of the door and shut it behind her gently. At least her mother's replies had been longer than two sentences. She even cried and that told her she was terribly sorry. He should have thought about it and realized she was telling the truth. How could he deny the truth? Before another breath was wasted, she backed out of the driveway and drove to her mother's house.

Chapter 5

When she reached her mom's house, she noticed a Black Maserati parked in the driveway. Not him, she thought to herself, please don't let it be him. She parked her car and then stared at herself in the mirror. "At least I don't look like a complete train wreck." She whispered. She got out of her car carefully and elegantly strolled to the door opening it. The house was silent.

"Mom? Where are you?" she yelled around the house.

She threw her keys onto the table and eyed the couch only to flop onto it unceremoniously. Her skirt rode up past her kneecap and she pulled it down with a quick tug. She heard footsteps heading towards her and stood up to face the culprit. He hadn't changed a bit and yet he did so much.

That beautiful black hair she had run her fingers through long ago was stylishly cut. His deep brown eyes glittered with amusement and held that conceited essence she had remembered so well. Her gaze went down to his lips which she had reminisced kissing her lips and neck. His trim body had filled in from his boyish figure. Tristan was anything but a boy now. She thought about how it would have felt if he wrapped his arms around her like he had many times before.

Aurora crossed her arms in front of her and felt her heart race frantically. Of course, he had to still be amazingly attractive. Time had done him well. Finally, she noticed she had been staring for a long time and averted her gaze to her feet. She heard his silky, husky chuckling as he stepped toward her. Damn him…

Her first instinct was to step back but instead, she held her ground.

"How are you, Aurora?" Tristan said smoothly.

Aurora thought her heart had come to a standstill. His voice was like that forbidden fruit she had wanted to indulge on for so long. She cleared her throat and held her composure.

"I'm doing perfectly Tristan," Aurora said with ease.

He smiled and she felt her heart pound yet again.

"That's good to hear," he said with a gentle smile.

The tension was thick between them. Aurora felt her mouth tug into a smile, and she started walking toward the kitchen. If her mom had set this up, she would have been upset. Or would she be thankful? Tristan had indeed been a surprise, but she didn't know if it was a good or bad one. She felt his gaze follow her as she walked away. Behind her, she heard a deep sigh and footsteps trailing her.

Her mom was in the kitchen humming a soft tune while cooking something. It smelled quite delicious, and she was shocked that her mom was cooking. They had always had a cook come in and make something when she was younger. Her mom turned to her and smiled.

"Hello dear. How was it at Dad's?" Maria said happily.

Aurora's mood darkened as her mother mentioned him. Tristan walked up and sat on a nearby stool.

"Horrible. He didn't listen to me. He didn't believe he was a bad father. You took it better than he did. He didn't even think about it that much. He just went to the damn conclusion he was a great dad." Aurora said heatedly.

Tristan listened in on this harsh conversation. He knew how hurt Aurora had been in the past and maybe in the present about her family. He saw how every day at school her smiles seemed forced. He had the picture-perfect family life everyone would have envied for, but he didn't bring it up around her. He valued her too much then to hurt her so stupidly. Now as he watched her speak so angrily about her father it pained him more to see her look so impassive. Those ten years had done a lot for her. Good and bad.

When he first saw Aurora all the guilt he had from before crept up on him. Those shining sky-blue eyes had darkened as they talked about this topic, but he remembered how bright they had been. He had to admit her voice was sweet and yet so strong. Her soft skin had a healthy glow upon it. He remembered that dark hair. It always seemed to be wild like her personality.

She was fire and he knew he would be burned by it but in the end, it was him who used her flame against her. She was so beautiful then, but now she had grown into a flawless being. So independent and natural it scared him still how her personality and looks affected him. Her personality held that hurt she recently carried the most, which he hoped didn't include seeing him. Maria turned to her daughter and frowned.

"John Mathews never changes. He's always been so damn stubborn. It was always what he wanted. Maybe this is why our family never worked out." Her mother murmured.

Aurora stared out the small window at the dark clouds that rolled along lovely weather for her horrible mood. "Well, Aunt Victoria and Dawn were there. This may make me sound childish but I'm jealous of Dawn. Dad treats her better than he treated me." Aurora said sadly.

Tristan felt his heart lurch painfully as he heard of her father's actions. Aurora was always a strong girl. She left this place just as he had. That itself was a strong move.

"That's his way. Don't let it phase you." Her mother said nonchalantly.

Without another word, Aurora departed the kitchen and headed to her old room. Tristan wanted to follow her, but Maria suggested he shouldn't.

"Tristan if you want to get close to her again then take it slow. I'm still working on that relationship with her. You hurt her a lot and so did I. We have to work at it for a while." She said with a gentle smile.

Tristan didn't know what to say so he decided to nod slowly and just sat there waiting for her to come back. Aurora ran up to her room as fast as she could. She needed to get away from this old feeling. The one that made her angry and the one that caused her grief when she least needed it. She wanted things to be better. Her life in Miami was working out for her but she had that feeling in her that needed to be appeased. Before she entered her room, she looked at the door.

On the door, she had left pictures and signs saying she was normal. She turned the knob slowly and entered the room and her past flashed before her. This was where the tears were shed, the laughs were let go, the screams were muffled from her ears, and the thoughts of a better life led her to reality. This room was her sanctuary when things had become harder. The beige walls had been covered with posters and pictures of her friends. In that room, all of her teenage belongings remained.

When she left, she decided to change her lifestyle. She didn't want to be treated as a child anymore. She wanted the maturity of everything to finally sink in. It did happen. She went to college, and culinary school, and then went to work for a famous restaurant. She didn't know if that maturity was all in her head or was there. I'm done with this place, she thought solemnly; after I'm gone it will be as if this place never existed yet again.

She roamed throughout the room and viewed the pictures hanging on the wall. There had been one picture that caught her eye and made her remember those things that happened years ago. It was her and Tristan. On that day, the sun was brighter than it had ever been, and they decided to go to the park. They sat on a swing together as she sat on his lap, and he kissed her. It was innocent but sparked unspeakable passion.

The picture was taken exactly when he kissed her by one of their friends. She was happy she got to look at the picture once again to see the memories that she had somewhat forgotten. She didn't know why she had forgotten that moment even if Tristan wasn't a big part of her life anymore. Her thoughts were broken after hearing a knock behind her. She turned around to see him leaning against the door jam. She smiled at him and lightly waved him in. This was the boy who had broken her very vulnerable heart, yet she had no room to hate him. He was also the one who had taught her what true love was. Frankly, it was too late for her to care. Love if wanted, would have been hard to refresh. They couldn't just start where they left off. What made it worse was she couldn't deny her renewed attraction for him. She was being affected by their past…their closeness…their intimacy.

He moved toward her and sat on the bed as she overlooked him. The last thing she needed was for Tristan to ruin her again.

"So, what do you do now and where do you live?" He questioned with a smile.

"I'm a Chef in Miami." She replied.

He chuckled. "I didn't see that coming." he said smiling wide.

Aurora raised an eyebrow and replied, "I decided to do it after college. Maybe I could have been a lawyer if I wanted to, but it wasn't me."

Tristan stared up at her and looked as she gave a faraway look. "Well, I bet you're a good chef." He spoke.

She looked down at him and replied, "I hope to think so." From the kitchen, Maria shouted to them and told them to come down for dinner.

Before Tristan moved out the door he stopped and looked back at her.

"You know I never wanted to hurt you." He whispered.

She stood in place and observed him. "It's all right Tristan. That's the past and I'm over it." She said straightforwardly.

He gaped at her for a minute before forcing a smile and departing down the hall. She groaned. What made him think she wanted to discuss the matter? It had embarrassed her and hurt her at the same time. He functioned as if nothing happened between them. If only he knew all thing things she felt about them. If he didn't mean to hurt, her what was that stunt he pulled supposed to do? Make her smile? She sat in her thoughts for minutes more before heading down the stairs to join them.

Chapter 6

Dinner went along without problems and their evening lasted with an easy conversation. After dinner, he got ready to leave. They said their goodbyes to their guest and Tristan said he would see Aurora the next day. As he left, Aurora went to get her suitcases in the car. She hurriedly went to her car and got all she needed. Her mom had said good night to her and kissed her hesitantly on the cheek. This gesture warmed Aurora's heart. Her mom was trying, and it was good enough for her.

As Aurora finished bringing all she wanted into her room, she slipped into the bathroom and took a relaxing bath. She thought back on her bittersweet day. She pondered about how the next day would be when she would see all those old faces. Nostalgia would be a big focus in this get-together. She didn't know if it was good or not.

As Tristan drove off into the night his thoughts came back to Aurora. He didn't know what his reason was for ditching her ten years ago on that day. He thought it was because he was scared. She was so headstrong. He was scared that she would hurt him so badly and yet he realizes he turned out to do that very fear to her. It had always bothered him because, after a fleeting time, he realized that it was the biggest mistake of his adolescent life. When he wanted to fix it, it was too late. Aurora left the town without a goodbye to anyone or signs of where she was going. It was only after a while he decided to leave this heartbreaking town himself. He moved to Philly and became a doctor. He knew what he wanted in his life, and nothing would stop him.

Time passed and he received a message from an old friend that Aurora had moved to Miami. There were rumors also that she was engaged to a man she fell in love with, but they quickly died out. His heart quivered as he heard this news, and he wanted to go see her for himself, yet he couldn't. What if she was actually getting married or just dating a guy? He didn't want to go there, seek her out, and then lose his chances when a man told him he was with her. Tristan groaned. He had already vowed to himself he wouldn't go down this road anymore.

He knew it was dangerous to risk his old yet renewed love for her. Truthfully there had never been a woman like her. She was smart, beautiful, witty, and humorous. All the rest of them were whiny, brainless, and money hungry. Even his current fling was the same. Her constant ranting was driving him insane, and he didn't know why he was putting himself through it.

He wanted to be with Aurora. He remembered how she used to smile. Those big eyes of hers brightened with her whole face. He felt horrible that he took her ability to smile away from her. As he spent those couple of hours with her, her smiles were very scarce. While Aurora was here, he planned to spend that time with her. He intended to win her back, but he had to take it slow. She was his muse to work harder but he knew the Aurora he knew before was different from now. Now she was a stranger to him. He groaned unhappily as he thought of her yet again. He knew he wasn't going to get any sleep at all tonight.

Chapter 7

The next morning as she woke up Aurora stared at the ceiling. As she looked up, she smiled lightly. This was it the day of the reunion. She got out of her bed and walked sleepily down the stairs. The smell of coffee made her giddy and she walked faster. As she entered the kitchen, she saw her mom humming yet again and pouring coffee into a big mug. As her mom heard her come in, she smiled and greeted her. Aurora sat on a stool and watched as her mom moved around the kitchen dizzily.

"Mom I'm going to do a little running around today and later on I'm going to my high school reunion." she said enthusiastically.

Maria looked at her daughter as she smiled wide. She hadn't seen her smile in so long. Truthfully, she hadn't even remembered when the last time was.

"Well, that's good. You haven't seen those people in a long time. It's time to show them how beautiful you turned out to be. They're going to be so star-struck." Her mom said giddily.

Aurora stared as her mother moved around her animatedly. This is it, she thought, today is the day you show them all you're still here.

"Thanks, Mom. By the way, did you invite Tristan here last night?" she said curiously.

Her mom smiled at her sheepishly. "I'm guessing you're upset about it?" her mom said.

Aurora shrugged. "Not really. I was just shocked really. I mean Tristan and I had a past that didn't end so great, but it was nice seeing him." Aurora said plainly.

Maria smiled at her daughter yet again. "You know you've become very mature," Maria said calmly.

Aurora looked up at her mom and thought about her comment. Had she become that mature? She hoped so. Aurora left the kitchen with a smile. She headed to her room and tossed her suitcases onto her bed. She couldn't decide what to wear. Truthfully, all those girls she had spent time together with in high school were fit to be models. She knew she couldn't compete with them now, but she decided she had changed. She waltzed to her wall full of pictures and viewed her old friends.

There was Roxy who always thought she was the outcast of their group. She was nothing near it. The little brunette had been shy and probably never changed. The boys came knocking on her door quicker than ever, but she still never felt confident with herself. Next Jen: was so full of joy and happiness that sometimes it was too hard to resist smiling along with her. Alexa was the other firecracker in the group. She might as well have had no shame or humility. She didn't listen to anyone. She usually flipped them off and screamed some curse at them while everyone just watched. She was loud and reckless yet had a heart of gold. Her looks were sharp and set to kill. Then there was Tina. She was the mom of the group. If any of them had boy problems Tina was the first one, they would consult with. She was pretty but didn't believe anyone who said so. Hopefully, Mr. Right had found her and drilled in her head the knowledge that she wasn't ugly. Together they were an interesting group.

Each one of them was different from the other. Aurora wished they hadn't changed as she had. She moved to her other pictures of her close friends who were guys. Anthony was the boy next door her whole adolescent life. He was that guy she might accidentally tell all her secrets to without caring. He was that close of a friend. He had that feeling around him that made her calm. He looked like any average, yet not average, boy. Dark hair and big brown eyes topped off with his lean body. Too bad Tristan was even more amazing. Anthony was drool-worthy. Her next friend was Max. He was that guy you would never expect to be a jock. He was kind of nerdy with glasses to top it off, but no one messed with him. Before senior year he had gotten contacts that made him look godly.

Aurora had to help him beat off girls once too many times. He could shoot hoops, score a touchdown, and hit a home run faster; he was the MVP they all loved. That was why Aurora had loved competing against him. She was competitive and so was he. Jack was the next exciting friend. He was an artist. He was enthralled by drawing scenic things and was quite amazing at it too. He was shy but a big softy when it came to romantic things. Aurora had to admit it was fun to be with him and be his muse for his drawings.

Ah, friendship was such a wonderful thing. Her world full of indignant people melted away as she spent time with these people. Tristan was part of their group. That was how she fell for him. Knowing him for all that time she knew more about him than anyone. She moved away and a fuzzy feeling expanded in her stomach. Within hours she would show them, and she became what she wanted. She wasn't that naïve little girl they were so used to anymore. It was her time to be on top of the world.

Chapter 8

Aurora rummaged through her bags and looked for a dress. She didn't think she needed a dress set to kill for her trip home but brought one anyway. Thankfully, she did, without knowing her desperate need for it. She pulled out a black silk dress with an elegant Sakura design on the side. She smiled mischievously and got dressed. She went to her full-length mirror and looked. The dress fit like a glove, and she loved how it looked. She sighed happily and couldn't wipe her devilish grin off her face.

The clock struck twelve and her anticipation level went higher. She pulled her heels on and went to fix her hair. In the past, her hair had been an unruly mess of curls, but she had let Renee fix her up like a Barbie. Now her hair was pin straight with bangs somewhat covering her face on the left side. She had to admit she looked flawless. She applied a little makeup that was only lip gloss, mascara, and eyeliner. She grabbed her bag, keys, jacket, and phone before taking one last look at herself in the mirror. She held onto the door frame and smiled at herself yet again.

She quickly walked down the stairs and heard her mother watching TV. It made her happy that she could spend minutes with her mom without realizing how hurt she was in the past. This was the relationship she wanted. She walked to the living room and sat next to her mom who turned out to be watching a soap opera. She heard her mom sniffling beside her and she rolled her eyes. Renee did the same thing. She would lie on the couch of their house and watch her little shows. Sometimes she would babble about how this one had been deprived of seeing that one and send herself into a crying streak. Aurora thought it was sadder to watch her cry over something as silly as those TV shows. Renee needed a boyfriend to tear her away from that crap.

If only, Aurora thought to herself with a smile. She couldn't manage Renee's ways maybe a guy would have gotten crazy being around her. She was so unorthodox. She heard her mom sniffle louder and she turned to face her. She knew Renee and her mom would like each other and mostly talk about mushy romantic crap while Aurora stayed in the room.

"Mom you're getting your shirt wet." she said jokingly.

Maria turned to her and frowned. Before Aurora knew it her mom threw a pillow at her. Aurora caught the pillow and laughed, her lungs constricting painfully. Her mom frowned and turned her attention back to the TV. Aurora found herself looking towards the TV just as some actors kissed.

"Uh mom, why were you crying if they were going to kiss? Isn't that a good thing?" She questioned.

"It's because they just realized they loved each other. It's so touching." Her mom said before transferring into a bawling mess. Aurora sat and rolled her eyes.

If this was the woman who gave birth to her, then from whom did she inherit her strong demeanor? Aurora looked at the wall clock and decided to leave.

"Wish me luck, mom. I get to meet up with old faces." she said giddily.

Maria smiled at her display and waved her daughter goodbye. Aurora entered her car and brought it to life. She glanced out the window and looked up at the barely blue sky. She knew it wouldn't rain but the sky had many fluffy white clouds covering any sign of blue. To Aurora, it was a beautiful day. She backed out of the driveway and drove to her old high school.

As she drove through the town, she looked at old places she spent time in. There were her friend's houses and those places she spent time together at. She passed by the old park where that picture of her and Tristan was taken and felt a chill run down her spine. She slowed down while viewing a group of teens laughing and hugging on the cool grass field. It reminded her of before. She drove off quickly, shaking her thoughts away. Before she knew it, she had reached the school. It looked the same. The boring gray paint had lost its glow since it had been newly painted when she graduated.

A big gym, a football field, a soccer field, a basketball court, and buildings made for classrooms. It was indeed a big school. Nostalgia kicked in and she quickly brought herself to reality. She parked her car in the parking lot she recalled kissing Tristan for the first time. It was while he sat on the hood of his truck. She had gotten so jealous of all those girls saying how nice it was to kiss him since he was a player. She was scared he would dump her soon, so she went for it. Little did she know Tristan was willing to stick around as long as it took just to be with her.

It was so embarrassing, but their kiss was steamy and lasted a good, solid two minutes. It wasn't her first kiss, but it was more gut-wrenching. She groaned to herself back to reality and got out of her car. She took a deep breath and strutted toward the gym. There was a huge banner that said Welcome Back Class of 1993. She felt her belly do another flop and with all her willpower she entered the school gym, even more nervous than she thought she would be.

Chapter 9

As she entered, she took note of the red and black balloons before looking at the people. The loud voices of her old classmates died out and all eyes were on her. She heard whispers of people who didn't believe that she was there. She felt herself become self-conscious and noticed a group of people rush toward her. It was Roxy, Jen, Alexa, and Tina followed by Jack, Max, and Anthony.

Wow, it had been so long. They all looked so different in the best way possible.

"AURORA!!!" Jen said while running as fast as her feet could take her.

Before she knew it, she practically tackled her with a vicious hug. All of them took their turns hugging and they smiled at her. She thought their smiles would wear out, but they hadn't. Aurora felt all her insecurities die down as did so. Anthony was the last to hug her and he held on tightly. She looked up into his eyes and felt her cheeks redden. She thought he was beyond gorgeous, but he hadn't sparked that fire she desperately needed to feel again. He had always looked boyish, and he still did but with a manly twist.

"You look great Aur." He said in a low whisper.

She laughed and replied, "Flattery must have gotten you everywhere."

All of them laughed and Roxy decided to speak up.

"I can't believe you're here!! When did you get here? Where do you live now? What do you do? Come on Aur, spill all you got! You have ten years' worth of things to tell us about!!" Roxy said with a big smile.

"I live in Miami and drove up here yesterday and I work for a big restaurant. It's adventurous over there." She said grinning from ear to ear.

It was time for Max to talk and he said, "No kidding. It's better than this boring old place! You still play sports?"

Aurora couldn't help but keep smiling. "I can't live without sports! I guess you're still showing people your unique abilities?" she said with a raised eyebrow.

"Yeah, I tend to shock people still not to brag or anything. I'm the head coach of this high school's basketball, football, and baseball team. Enough about me, tell us about your life! Find that dream guy you used to tell me about?" he said grinning. Aurora laughed loudly.

"No, I haven't but I was close. I just couldn't keep up with his reputation as everyone's golden boy. I bet you guys read that in the paper." she said, thinking back to Mike Roberts.

"Yes!! I did oh my god that was a really massive thing!!" Alexa piped up happily.

"I thought people didn't care that much for him," Aurora said shocked.

"It was quite big here and also about your engagement to him real or a rumor?" Jack said with a devilish grin.

"It was real, but I couldn't keep up with the blah... blah besides I'm still young and I'm not in a rush to get married," Aurora said while all of them looked at her outraged.

"You were about to get married to Mike Roberts and you didn't tell any of us anything??? What the hell were you thinking?" Tina said with a smirk.

"I don't think I was thinking!! It was so fast, but we went out for seven months before he asked." Aurora said loudly.

"So that means at the moment you're single?" Anthony said lastly.

"Yes, I am, and I plan to stay so for now." she said firmly.

She looked at them and their smiles looked as if they were plastered onto their faces.

"What about you guys? Are any of you married yet?" Aurora said curiously.

Tina blushed and looked over at Jack who did the same. "Actually, uh Tina and I are getting married next month," Jack said while rubbing his head.

"Really? That's great you guys!!! You can fill me in on all the details later!" Aurora said happily.

"Thanks, Aur," Tina said with a shy smile. "Any more of you getting married? Or dating anyone I should know about?" Aurora said in a motherly tone.

Roxy blushed and turned to Anthony as he did the same.

"We're dating." They said together while pointing at each other.

Aurora laughed at the display and congratulated them. Before anyone else was able to say any more Tristan walked up to them. Everyone greeted him and turned to Aurora to see if the tension was thick between them.

"Hello, Tristan," Aurora said smiling. He leaned in for a hug and she gave him one back. He smelled so good it was almost sinful. To Aurora, he was amazingly handsome at that moment. He wore a button-down shirt under his dress jacket. His jeans made him look interesting as they came in contrast with his top. He was delicious and he knew it.

"Hey Aurora, how's it going?" he said smoothly. She looked up to his eyes and they glittered furiously.

"Amazing. How about you?" she said dragging their conversation longer.

"Great." He smirked suspiciously.

Everyone around them stared with suspicious looks but dropped it knowing they had not been entirely anxious around each other. They finally sat at a table. The gym was where they had their school dances, and she thought back on how people danced on that same dance floor back then. Before she knew it, her friends had been pulled out to the dance floor with smiles. Aurora sat at the table alone and within minutes a familiar guy walked up to her.

"Would you like to dance?" he asked.

Aurora looked up at him and watched as his blue eyes glittered. "Only if you tell me your name first." She flirted slightly.

"I'm Mark. We had some classes together I think." He said with a faraway look.

"Mark Webber. I remember you." She said with a really big smile. Mark had been her lab partner for a long time in chem. He was cute, she had to admit but it was just looks and she had seen better ones.

"I'm honored." He said while grabbing her hand to pull her up. She stumbled slightly and he caught her without a problem.

"Careful there don't fall for me too quickly." He said teasingly.

She laughed without trying to stop herself. It was a cheesy line and truthfully, she loved it. He pulled her onto the dance floor, and they danced slowly to the gentle music. When the song ended, he departed from her and Aurora was left yet again at a table. She viewed the happy faces of everyone and smiled thinking of their happiness. Suddenly she felt a hand touch her bare arm from behind and she turned around. It was Tristan.

She motioned to a seat, and he took it. For him, it was one of the hardest times ever. Watching her dance in that dress with Mark annoyed him to no end but he knew he couldn't do anything about it. If he did, it would cause a big scene and ruin everything he was planning. The dress was practically made for her and yet also made for his enjoyment. The black fabric used for the dress brought out her eyes and complimented her dark hair. It clung to her body like a glove and his eyes scanned her unconsciously.

C'mon Tristan. Get it together. You're twenty-seven not seventeen anymore, he thought firmly. He noticed he had been staring at her involuntarily and she looked at him with a flushed face. Aurora was shocked as he stared at her. He made her feel as if she were a specimen under a microscope. He used to do that a lot. His eyes penetrated her heart and seemed to see what all her secrets were. It made her feel fuzzy inside and yet she couldn't let it get to her. She couldn't and yet it already had gotten to her.

Her mind was telling her to go for it and forget everything that happened between them, but her heart recalled the pain that he caused and ached feverously. What she wanted was to forgive and forget but it was impossible. Tristan could tell she had been in deep thought so he sat back watching the couples sway to the sweet music. He eyed Tina and Jack somewhat jealously and caught them smiling at each other.

They had dated during their second year of college and all of them except Aurora and Tristan had gone to. Now, years later they were getting married and always looked as if they were in a blissful dream that never ended. If things hadn't turned out the way they had, he and Aurora would have been as such. It was his fault, and he knew it, but she was also to blame. Before all of them noticed, the reunion had ended, and it was time to head home. Everyone said their goodbyes to each other but knew they would have seen each other around the town.

Aurora didn't want the night to end. This had been the first time in a while that she had been with the people she had always been close to and the first time in forever that she had just relaxed. All of her friends agreed to have a get-together sometime during her stay. Aurora was excited and they all said their goodbye. She walked to her car and heard rustling behind her. She didn't know who it was, and she didn't care before turning around.

Chapter 10

It was Mark. Aurora didn't know what to think. Was he following her? She mentally scolded herself for being paranoid, but she knew the possibilities were endless. He did flirt with her and during their dance; his hands traveled a bit too much.

"Hey Aurora wait up!!" she heard behind her as Mark caught up to her. She didn't want to be rude, but she wanted nothing but to tell him to go away.

"Hey Mark, what's up?" she said while turning to face him.

"I just wanted to ask you if you would like to go for dinner sometime while you're here." He huffed out.

She was shocked. This wasn't what she was expecting while she was here. It was a good shock, but she felt queasy about it. She didn't want to say yes and yet she couldn't bring herself to say no. He was good-looking and had a great personality. What would go wrong? She silently cursed herself for jinxing her chances at it but knew she couldn't go through with it.

"I'm sorry Mark. I can't." she said sadly. Mark looked at her dejectedly and quickly smiled to cover it.

"Don't worry about it. I'm a big boy and I could take it." He said assuredly. She quickly hugged him and told him it was great to see him. "The pleasure was all mine." He said bowing goofily.

He walked off and Aurora walked to her car as fast as her feet took her. She got to her car and threw her bag into the passenger seat. She closed the car door and strolled to the hood of the car. She sat on the hood observing the school while everyone else drove away. The wind blew softly, and her hair whipped onto her face. That was the end of the most pondered day. She chuckled lightly at the thought of this old home of hers. She stared once more into the bright sky and turned away before entering her car.

It had been an interesting night and yet she couldn't grasp the fact that she had left this part of her life that was the only part that made her happy. Then again, she had troubles in her home here, so it was best to leave. 'No regret,' she thought boldly. 'Don't regret it.'

The next day, Aurora went for a quick run around the neighborhood to be stopped more than once by the residents of their gated community. All those elderly people she had helped during her high school days stared at her with the same awestruck expression she had gotten so used to. 'There's nothing special about me. Just little Aurora Mathews who grew up, she thought.

When she got back to her house there was a new car parked in the driveway. Another visitor I wondered who it was this time, she thought somewhat scared. She entered the house and bellowed to her mom.

"Hey mom where are you?" she yelled continuously.

Her mom didn't answer, and she looked around for signs of her mom. She looked into the dining room and saw Maria sitting with a young woman whose back was facing her, so she didn't know who it was. The woman turned and Aurora gasped happily.

"Renee, didn't I tell you to not come up here?" Aurora laughed at full volume. Renee stood up and ran full speed at her.

"I know but I had to come!! You left all of a sudden and I got bored and lonely. It hasn't been the same since Nick left me. I tried getting a rebound at the bar yesterday, but it didn't work." Renee said in her signature pouty voice. To think they were best friends. They were nothing alike.

"Well, I'm happy you're here. I get to introduce you to everyone here since they're all within walking distance." Aurora said excitedly.

"This is so exciting!! I have to admit this town is cute! And speaking of cuties, this town is full of them! You look a lot like your mommy Aur." Renee hadn't expected that her best friend would look too similar to her mom. They would have passed as sisters since she was quite young. Aurora smiled and hugged her friend. Aurora turned to her mom who raised an eyebrow at her. She smiled sweetly at her and tossed Renee a look. She turned to her mom again and pulled Renee out of the awkward room and up the stairs. She dragged Renee to her room, and she stumbled more than once at the sudden lurches.

When they were in the sacred sanctuary of her room Renee pointed to a picture and smiled.

"Who's this hottie?" She said in a low tone.

Aurora walked up to the wall and looked at the picture of Tristan and her at their junior prom. "Tristan Alvarez my first love and possibly last," Aurora said sadly.

Renee's eyes widened with shock. "So that's him? The guy who broke the heartbreaker's heart? Interesting, I have to admit he is quite the looker." She said with a devious smile.

Aurora rolled her eyes and said, "Don't worry he's part of your town tour." Renee laughed and looked at the picture of Aurora and Tristan at the park. To her, they looked like they were in love. Even if it was just puppy love, it was love. Now, Aurora didn't show that happiness that had been displayed in the photo while he had been around.

Maybe he was that final piece Aurora needed in her life. She just didn't know it yet. Her eyes had sparkled into that light and bright blue Renee herself, as

Aurora's best friend, had only seen once or twice. She remembered how Aurora had explained their breakup. Her friends here knew he had ditched her on that night and that was true. Aurora had left out a big part in that explanation. He had told her he loved her and dropped her. His excuses built up and she thought it was because he was cheating on her. Luckily, it wasn't but his love only lasted in words.

From the time before their anniversary, he had already decided she wasn't the one for him. She skimmed more pictures and most of them were of her and her old friends at parties, picnics, dances, and just hanging out at her house. It reminded Renee of her old high school days, and she smiled at the thought. Aurora had been a happy teen, but Renee knew it was only at school. When she arrived home there was either complete silence or uncontrollable screaming. It wasn't a life for a perfectly happy girl. Without knowing who she was or how her life was you would have known she had been deeply hurt by the ones she thought loved her. When Renee met Aurora in their first week of college, she knew that Aurora had demons in her past that she couldn't let go of. That's what made her intriguing. Renee looked over a picture with Aurora arm in arm with three boys who were each handsome with no debate.

They all had wide smiles and there was one guy with glasses that looked like he had just come out of a magazine. The glasses took nothing away from his good looks and in other pictures with him, he might have had contact lenses. To Renee, he had the most incredible eyes. It sounded cliché but those eyes seemed to have their own story, and they were calling to her.

"Who is this guy?" Renee asked with awe.

She looked closely at the picture and then back at Renee with a big grin.

"Why does it matter?" She replied still grinning.

"Look at him Aur!! He's so gorgeous! Plus, those eyes! I think I could stare at them all day." Renee said dreamily. Aurora laughed at Renee's display and sat on her bed. "That is my dear friend Max. Best athlete in school besides me and an overachiever. Excellent choice sweetie." Aurora said happily.

Renee turned her attention once more to the picture. "Is he part of our tour?" she asked hopefully.

"Only if you're a good girl," Aurora said.

"I promise I will be as long as I get to meet that hottie," Renee said with genuine determination.

Aurora laughed at her and quickly pulled out her suitcases. "Okay first help me to find something to wear. Then I promise I will try my best to help you with Max." Aurora said with a smile.

Renee rolled her eyes and helped Aurora with her apparel. "Now I have the feeling you're just using my newfound crush for your gain." Renee frowned.

Aurora laughed and threw a sock at her. "Well don't think like that. I'm going to make Max like you, and he won't even know what hit him." Aurora said while her friend watched her suspiciously.

"I trust you," Renee said with a big smile.

Chapter 11

Within thirty minutes, Renee had dressed Aurora in a fashionable yet comfortable way. They went down the stairs with fluttering smiles and looked for Maria throughout the house. They walked into the living room and Maria was watching her soaps yet again. Renee watched as Maria bawled on the couch loudly. Aurora rolled her eyes at her mother and Renee grinned wide.

"Is that what I look like while I watch those shows?" Renee whispered.

Aurora turned to her with a knowing look. "No dearest. You look more pathetic than that." Aurora said with a big smile. She frowned and shoved Aurora lightly. As Aurora laughed uncontrollably, Renee walked and flopped onto the couch. Maria looked up at Renee with a smile and started crying again. Maria curled up against Renee and she patted her gently to calm her. She turned to Aurora who tried her best to stifle her laugh but ended up cracking only seconds later. After the cheesy episode Aurora and Renee left Maria to her agenda. They left the house with even bigger smiles and a mission.

They got into Aurora's car and Aurora pulled out her phone. She dialed a number and put the phone to her ear.

"Hey, Ant it's Aur can you bring the group to the diner? In about thirty? Yes, even Tristan if you want. I'm all right with him now. Long story but I want to introduce you all to my best friend. Don't worry, no one could replace you stud. Oh, you're good. See ya when I see ya." Aurora said with pauses between each reply from Anthony. Renee turned to her with a questioning look.

"I don't think I can trust you anymore. You're going to let me meet all of them at once? I feel more nervous than when we went to class." Renee said shakily.

Aurora rolled her eyes. "Don't be, they're not that bad. You're going to love them." She scoffed. Aurora turned on her car and they backed out of the driveway.

"Who's Ant? Is he one of the guys in the picture?" Renee asked. Aurora thought back to the picture.

"Yeah, he was the dark-haired big brown eyes. Besides Max, those boys are taken by some other girl in my group. So luckily you chose my single boy." Aurora said with a big smirk.

"Your boy? Are you his mother or something?" Renee laughed happily.

"No, I can't be his mom, but he's like a brother to me though so if you break his fragile big boy heart, I might burn your Prada purse at home." Aurora threatened happily.

Renee feigned mock horror and replied, "I haven't even met the guy yet. What makes you think we're going to get together?"

Aurora gave her a significant look. "Please, you'll have him eat out of the palm of your hand within seconds of knowing you." She replied with a snort.

Renee smiled deviously and replied, "Not seconds, give it two minutes."

As they drove off to the diner Aurora felt her heartbeat somewhat furiously. She was going to see Tristan yet again. She had already seen him twice while she was here, but she still felt overly self-conscious.

"Hey Aur, are you okay? You look like you're about to tear the wheel off." Renee said eyeing her friend's knuckles turning white.

"Yeah, why? Do I look like I'm stressed?" she asked while her eyes started tearing up.

"Sweetie, your knuckles are turning white from gripping onto that wheel. You look like you're going to strangle it. Of course, you look stressed." She replied sensitively.

Aurora pouted and pulled up into the diner's parking lot. She turned off her car and looked over at her friend. "I'm nervous about Tristan even if I've seen him twice already. I never feel this way about other guys, it's only him and yet I can't let go of the past. He doesn't love me." she admitted.

Renee turned to her friend and watched as she looked around distressed. "Do you think you still possibly love him? I know it may seem bizarre to you since you don't want to fall in love again and go through any of this again but think about it. You can't stop thinking about him, and you get nervous at the thought of seeing him, it looks as if you are confessing to murder right now from the look on your face and I'm pretty sure you're thinking of all those little possibilities of him not breaking your heart in the first place. Am I right?" She said while Aurora furrowed her brows in thought.

"I don't know. That's slightly how I feel but it's not love. It's like a teenage crush that repeats itself. I've felt this way about him before and I know after what we've been through, it's not love. If I forgive him for before then I'll prove to be weak." she said hesitantly. Renee was surprised. Aurora talked to her about Tristan a lot, but she had never acted so vulnerable about the subject. Yes, it is love, she can lie to me all she wants, but it is so true, Renee thought smiling to herself.

"Whatever you wish to believe deary," Renee said while patting Aurora's knee softly. Aurora smiled watery at her and nodded slowly. They both stepped out of the car and Aurora felt all tension wash away.

From inside the diner, Tristan watched as Aurora and a girl sat in Aurora's car and talked. He watched closely as Aurora gripped onto the wheel and cried a bit. He felt his heart tighten and crush at the sight of her crying. She never cried around anyone even though she was going through the toughest things. That girl she was with must've been able to get into her heart. He watched them and suddenly felt someone tap him. He turned to see one of his closest friends, Jen, tower over him.

"Hey stranger, what's going on?" she said with a signature Jen smile.

He smiled back up at her and patted the seat next to him. She sat down with an even bigger smile and stared out the window. "Same old stuff. How about you?" he said while hugging her gently.

She punched him in the gut and still smiled innocently. "Oh, I'm all right but keep your hands off. You're looking at your ex's old friend here. Even if you're practically my brother, that fragile heart you broke is coming into this diner. Speaking of that particular lovely lady, who's the one next to her?" Jen said pointing to Aurora in her car.

Tristan looked back at the car and shrugged. "I think that's her best friend from Miami." Jen looked out the window as Aurora waved her hands around explaining something. She noticed Aurora had been crying a bit and Jen herself became shocked. Aurora never cried through all of it.

"Aurora never cries. I wonder what happened now." Jen said worried.

Tristan turned his attention to the almost vacant diner. It was his whole group without Aurora so far. The rest of them were playing pool next to their corner booth and laughing happily. Jack and Tina had their arms wrapped around each other and so did Anthony and Roxy. Tristan watched as Max rolled his eyes at them and Alexa talked on her phone to her boyfriend. He knew Max was waiting for that one girl to attract his attention. Tristan himself had witnessed girls by the tons throw themselves at Max. The guy didn't want any of them. It would only take a little more time before he would find that girl.

"So, Jen, do you have a boyfriend you aren't telling me about?" Tristan said with a smirk. Jen looked up at him and shrugged.

"My ex-boyfriend Steven dumped me last week in a text. He didn't want to be in a committed relationship, so I'm left to think, what's wrong with me? I'm getting really sad about it you know." Jen said, forcing some happiness into her words.

Tristan looked over at the girl next to him. "Nothing is wrong with you. It's what's wrong with them that you should look at. Never think it's you. Guys are shallow sometimes. Not Max, Anthony, Jack, or me though, we're the only good boys in your life." He said with a wink.

Jen smiled wide and punched Tristan in the arm. "No, I'm quite sure out of all the boys in the world you guys are at the bottom of the list for being good boys. I remember when Paul Johnson went out with Roxy, and he broke up with her in the middle of class. The next day you four boys went out to find him. You made Roxy happy. Paul was such an ass anyway. Luckily, she got Ant now." Jen pouted and leaned against Tristan.

He thought back on that event and remembered how sad Roxy was. When Jack suggested teaching the sucker a lesson, they all wanted in. They hadn't hurt him that badly, only one or ten bruises and a cut lip. Yeah…no different.

Chapter 12

As Aurora and Renee entered the diner everyone stared yet again except for all her friends. Alexa was on the phone but ended the call before looking up at Aurora. Just as Jen did last night, Alexa ran full speed at Aurora and engulfed her in a hug. Aurora laughed as Alexa practically carried her to the rest of the group.

Aurora looked as if the two couples were busy with each other's loving goodness. Max was watching as they did so and rolled his eyes with a smile.

"Hey you guys, look! Guess who I got!" Alexa said with a big smile.

Again, Aurora was trampled by them and before she knew it Anthony carried her to the pool table. He placed her on the table, and she punched him in the arm. "You're scaring my friend Ant," Aurora said jumping off the table and walking towards Renee.

"Aur, I uh should wait in the car. It's an old friend's reunion, not for me to barge in on." Renee said while Aurora pulled her hand toward the rest of the crowd.

"Stop being a baby. They're going to adore you." Aurora said while rolling her eyes.

As they reached everyone their eyebrows raised in question. "This is Renee, my closest friend from Miami," Aurora said while Renee blushed furiously. Jen stood up from her position next to Tristan and walked up to them.

"Hi, I'm Jen. It's great to meet you." She said with a big smile. Renee smiled and they got into a conversation. Aurora watched as Tristan sat in the corner drinking a beer looking out the window. Aurora walked over to Max, who was standing next to the couple. She grabbed him in for a hug and he looked down at her shocked.

"Hey Aur." He said with a grin. He leaned down to kiss her cheek, and she laughed sweetly.

"Hey Maxxy. Looks like you're still the charmer. How are you?" she said, smiling as he put his arm around her shoulders.

"Great now that you're here." he said with an arrogant grin.

Aurora rolled her eyes. "Please love. I eat guys like you for breakfast. Is that all you got? What happened to blowing the socks off me with your smooth ways?" Aurora said happily.

Max laughed loudly and tried to catch his breath. "I think you're mistaking me for Jack." He said with a big smile.

"Last I checked you used to do the same thing. That's why I had to beat off at least three girls a day for your sake." Aurora said with a scoff. Max rolled his eyes and thanked the world he had, Aurora. She was the sister he always wanted. He turned himself to the girl whom Aurora came in with. She was quite pretty. She had that look about her that she was innocent and vulnerable. Her smiles lit up her face and seemed to warm that snowy December day.

"So, tell me more about your friend," Max said with some nervousness.

Aurora untangled herself from him and smiled suspiciously. "Looks like Maxxy has a crush." She said in a sing-song voice.

"Maybe I do, maybe I don't," he said mocked back.

"She's a great girl Max. Dare I say perfect for you. Judging by what your type was in high school I think she fits your standards. She picked me up after breakups. They weren't fun, so she told me that I was perfect the way I was, and I shouldn't let anyone change my mind. Too bad none of the exes has ever said that." Aurora said gloomily.

Max looked down at his close friend and pulled her into a hug again. "Guys are stupid, and we make mistakes but those guys you've dated are incredibly ridiculous. They shouldn't have tried to change you. They should have just gotten to learn to love you for you. I know I have." Max said lightly.

Aurora looked up at him with a glint in her eye. "You topped off your charmer lines." She said with a grin. Max grinned and flicked her on her arm.

Tristan watched as Aurora and Max talked. When he kissed her on the cheek Tristan almost stood up. Her smiles as she talked to Max widened with each word said and he couldn't keep his arm off her. She wasn't even his anymore, so he knew he had no say in what she did. Tristan wanted to feel annoyed, but he couldn't. It was Max. He was harmless when it came to dating and anything that involved love. He also knew Max had different standards than most. He had met the girl Aurora brought with her and she smiled warmly at everything and even him. He could have sworn Aurora told this woman about their past and yet she was all smiles and warmth. Her eyes had a gleam in them that scared Tristan a bit. She seemed dynamic and that was perfect for her.

Truthfully, if time let them, Max and Renee were perfect for each other in Tristan's mind. He saw Max pull Aurora at arm's length and shake her a bit to knock some sense into her. Aurora smiled wearily and they continued with their conversation.

"So, Tristan, tell me about you," Renee said looking over at him. Tristan turned his body away from Max and Aurora and looked at the girl intently. He picked up his beer and shot back a couple of sips before answering.

"What's there to say? I'm from here and moved to Philly ten years ago but come back here occasionally. My girlfriend of a month is a snotty bitch who wants me to propose already but little does she know I lost interest in her three days into the relationship. I'm an easygoing guy and I love dogs." He said with a menacing smile.

Renee raised an eyebrow and chuckled. "Looks like you need more excitement in your life." She said with a grin.

"How about you? It doesn't look like you get any excitement in your life." Tristan said while leaning closer to the table.

"My life revolves around exciting things. I have to keep up with missed things over there. I'm from NYC so I like busy places. Now I live in Miami with Aurora and I'm her secretary. It's a tough job so I like it. My boyfriend just dumped me because he decided I was too determined for him. Turns out he was sleeping with the restaurant's lawyer's secretaries. His loss is my gain since I get to be independent, yet I still want that fairytale romance all women want at some point. I guess I should learn how to stop telling people my hopes and dreams since it'll turn out the way it did with the jerk." Renee admitted thoughtfully.

Tristan gazed at the woman gently. What was up with guys hurting the good women? They were ruining the image of all men. "I think that it's good when you tell people what you want in your life. It shows that you're already aiming for what you've always wanted. Don't give a shit about what people think. It should always be about what you want to happen and what you think is right for your life." Tristan spoke softly.

Renee was shocked. This guy was good. He knew what to say and when to say it. He had that feeling around him that made you feel so relaxed even if you hadn't known him that well. Renee knew this was one of the reasons Aurora loved him before. When she told her tale, he looked at her intently and seemed to understand what she was talking about. It was like she had known him forever. "Thanks, Tristan. You're a great guy." Renee said with a sincere smile.

He was stunned by her reaction. She smiled at him and said he was a great guy. He didn't think a girl could say that to him so naturally. Especially if they knew how he treated Aurora. "Thanks." He said with a smile.

Aurora sat with her friends and spent the day learning more about how everyone lived now. Jack was fulfilling his dream as a painter and was becoming a new fresh artist in the city. People loved his drawings and bought them rapidly which helped him. When his parents found out he wanted to be a painter, they were upset. They were both doctors of the area and wished their son to follow but he was too passionate about his drawings. They didn't know he would be a top painter and when they found out, they showed all the dismay they had. Now that he was about to marry Tina, they were extremely happy. Tina was a doctor in the hospital where his parents had worked. Their romance was off to a great start as both families agreed to it.

Anthony had become a teacher at their high school which shocked Aurora the most. He hadn't always been on top of his grades and now he was a

Chemistry teacher. He and Roxy had been dating since their second year of college and still going strong. Aurora thought that after Jack and Tina got married, Ant would have proposed to Roxy. Ant, being a good friend, didn't want to steal away their thunder. Roxy had also become a teacher at an elementary school.

Alexa had become a journalist for the NY Times. Aurora thought it was significant, thinking that she hated English class all her life. Her boyfriend was a businessman who traveled to various places. Their relationship must have been extraordinarily strong to think that they were okay with being apart. Alexa knew he wouldn't do anything to hurt her, so it was great for her.

Jen became a nurse. She was good at lightening up her patient's day since they were all children, it made it all the better. Aurora was happy that they all turned out successful and happy. She remembered how they used to tell each other about what they wanted to be. Aurora had always answered that she didn't know but found that cooking was relaxing and somewhat therapeutic. Aurora was happy once again to be around them and reminisced those times they had when they were younger.

Aurora looked at Renee and Tristan. They were in a deep conversation. She hoped they weren't talking about their past and knew Renee wouldn't bring it up. They smiled at each other and laughed happily as if they were old friends. Aurora smiled and felt a hand rub her back softly. She looked up and saw Jack smiling down at her flirtatiously.

"I miss you being around here." He said dramatically.

Aurora grabbed him for a hug and caught him off guard. "I missed you too Jack! I'm so happy you and Tina are getting married. I better be invited." Aurora smirked.

Jack pulled away from her and pulled a stray hair away from her face. "Aurora, would we tell you about the wedding if you weren't invited? Humm?" Jack smiled knowingly.

Aurora looked toward Tina who was dancing around with Ant as Roxy watched smiling. "You never know. I haven't seen you all in ten years, and I didn't even tell you guys I was leaving. Are you mad I didn't tell you?" She questioned nervously.

Jack's face darkened and he looked her straight in the eye. "I was but I got over it. We all talked about it when you left, and we decided that you were chasing your dream life. It was only after three weeks that we found out your parents divorced. Plus, we knew you had problems with Tristan and then your parents so we decided you did the best move you could think of." Jack said with a shrug.

She couldn't help but cry. She had become such a baby today. It wasn't normal for her to be such an emotional wreck. What he said was true. She wanted that life she dreamed about. She didn't let anything stop her and she didn't realize that she hurt the ones she loved. Jack pulled her into a hug while shushing her softly and she gave a watery laugh and said, "Don't worry Jack. I promise to tell you all where I am from now on."

Renee turned to view everyone and noticed Aurora crying softly into the guy who she thought was Jack. They were a close-knit group, and she could see why Aurora had held these people close to her heart.

"Hey Tristan, tell me more about Max." She said, turning towards Tristan, who was still sitting across from her. Tristan smiled at the flushed woman in front of him. "Looks like you have a crush, and you don't even know him." He smirked while looking towards Max.

He looked back at the woman who viewed him with wide eyes and a blushing face. "I uh well... I don't know." She stuttered uncomfortably.

He chuckled and leaned in closer to whisper to her. "Don't worry. I won't tell anyone about this little crush." He whispered with a wink.

Renee buried her face into her open hands and groaned. "I just want you to tell me about him," Renee said still blushing.

Tristan threw her a knowing look. "Sweety, you're practically drooling at the thought of him. It's not obvious but I'm good at knowing these things." He smiled smugly.

She gaped at him. "Wow. You're good." She sighed tiredly. "To answer that question earlier, he's a great guy. I've known him since he moved next door to me in second grade. It was nice since I finally had a friend my age in my neighborhood. I remember when we used to play sports he would be beyond best even if pissed everyone off, no one could mess with him. He is pretty smart which makes people envy him more but it's just more that he's an overachiever. It's really good to have someone like him around because he knows how to relax you." He smiled lightly.

Renee thought about that declaration. This Max guy was interesting. He intrigued her more than other guys did, and she loved how it felt to be thinking of a guy nonstop yet again. He seemed different from the superficial jerks she dated before and that was a good sign.

"Thanks, Tristan. You think I have a chance?" she asked grinning.

"Maybe." He said shrugging. They both laughed loudly and brought themselves back to reality.

"I feel like I'm a teenager telling my best guy friend back home about all my crushes and flings. He always told me about what guys want and I decided all guys are different and I shouldn't think they're all the same. Turns out they practically are." she admitted. Their conversation deepened and it felt as if they talked forever.

"I think you should talk to her for a bit," Aurora said as Max walked next to her. He rolled his eyes at her and smiled.

"Look Aur I'm a big boy and I can do this. No need to mommy me anymore. Plus, she seems interested in her talk with Tristan so why should I be rude and butt in?" Max said exasperated.

Now it was Aurora's turn to roll her eyes, and she laughed. "Well, if you don't want to talk to her now, you'll get other chances," Aurora said with a big smile. Max looked at her with a gleam in his eyes.

Chapter 13

As the day drew on Tristan had gotten to know the interesting, perky Renee over that brief time. He could see why Aurora had become her friend. This woman was interesting and dreadfully honest. She barely knew him and yet she was already talking about her past loves and her life in general. This girl had her share of bumps in the road which made Tristan more aware of a woman's mentality. 'I'm turning into a softie,' he thought to himself.

"So, Renee, Since Aurora doesn't plan on talking to me about her life how are things going with her?" he said.

She eyed him curiously and took a sip of her coffee. "Well, her fiancé and she broke it off about two weeks before the wedding. She was a bit heartbroken, but she already knew it would turn out that way because she couldn't stand the thought of commitment. I remember her telling me one night that he said he loved her. She told me she was scared at that moment, and it was because he was exactly everything she wanted. Too bad she couldn't keep up with him. They were a really happy couple. She smiled a lot around him but after they broke up it was weird since she made it seem like he never existed. I guess love works like that. The poor girl just wanted to drop it to get away from all the crap she was taking. Besides that, she's been great and successful. "Renee sighed as she thought back to the certain time.

She knew it wasn't the whole story, but Tristan was catching on. He smiled faintly and he couldn't help but think back to what she had just said. "So how long were they together?" He asked.

Renee bit her tongue. Her somewhat true speech was the perfect bait, and he got on… Hook, line, and sinker. It showed he still cared. "Well, they were together for about a couple of months before they got engaged. I barely saw her when he was in town. They were inseparable." Renee smirked.

Tristan frowned a bit annoyed and yet held his serenity. He couldn't let it be obvious. He had to lie low for a while since he still had to build his relationship with her up. She was such a hard shell to crack. He knew in the end, if luck was on his side, he'd be able to have his love with him. He groaned inwardly and braced his head on his hands. "Well, at least things were good for her in FL. I was worried that she'd do something reckless." he said, clearly impulsive in his words.

Renee stared at him until she was confident about her next reply. "She's not that kind of person. You should know that. You've known her longer than I have." she said with an annoying twist.

"Yeah, I know. I guess I was thinking about how she left here without mentioning anything and within a couple of weeks her parents divorced. I never heard from her until a couple of days ago." Tristan said wholeheartedly.

Renee remembered that time. Aurora had been a mess. She hadn't eaten or attended school that week. She was adamant towards everyone if she did step out of her room. "Well, if I were you, I'd pray she sticks around," Renee said before sipping her coffee again. Their conversation died out and they sat in a comforting silence for minutes more.

The fun night ended, and Aurora headed to her car forgetting she had Renee with her. Renee followed after her and they entered the car with smiles. Aurora opened her mouth to talk but Renee cut in. "You should have told me all of them looked amazing. I felt so out of place, and they all looked like they were on some TV show. I have to admit you have good taste in men. Tristan is a great guy. Too bad he was the one who screwed up." Renee said while whispering the last part as quietly as she could with Aurora still hearing her.

Aurora gripped the wheel strongly as she backed out of the parking spot. "Yeah, I know but let's talk about him later. Right now, I'm going to show you one of the best places in the world." she said dismissively.

Renee shrugged instinctively and turned on the radio. They drove along the road and Aurora pointed to various places where special memories were made. The whole time Aurora wouldn't say the person's name and Renee knew it was about Tristan. Renee knew they were close. Aurora had those memories of him, and it looked as if she didn't plan to let them go no matter how much they hurt her. They drove over a bridge and to the falls. The sun was barely setting over the horizon and the water was a piercing color.

"Wow. Aurora this place is amazing. I thought all sunsets were the same. This place is nothing near the typical beach." Renee said as she stepped out of the car.

Aurora looked out at the blazing sun and smiled. "I usually came here after school to think. My parents never cared anyway so I stayed there till sunset and the stars took their turn at the show. I loved being here." Aurora said hugging herself.

Renee turned away from her and cringed slightly. It was always hard for her to hear about Aurora's past. It was so sad to hear how a little girl could act so grown up and push all things in her life that hurt her away. She was forced to be an advanced girl from an early age and not have a childhood like her friends had. She never learned how to ride a bike from her dad or learn how to cook with her mom. She learned all those things on her own or with other people. She learned how to be independent since it was how she had to be. Through it all, she still managed to smile that big smile full of radiance. Nothing could stop that smile that already hadn't tried to.

"A lot of people care about you Aurora. You inspire them to keep going strong in their lives. Don't let the mistakes of your parents change you. Everyone who knows you hasn't once said they didn't need you. Even the ex! You guys were set to get married, and it didn't turn out the way, but the guy knew he couldn't let you out of his life. That's why he settled for friends. It shows people care tons about you." Renee said sharply.

Aurora tried to let those words sink in, but she couldn't. Even if she looked at it from Renee's point of view, she knew it wasn't entirely true. Her mom had said she cared about her only a few days ago and yet she had nothing to do with her for countless years before. She had decided to forgive and forget on her mother's part. "Thanks, Renee. You're a great friend." Aurora said while the breeze swished around her. Renee smiled.

They spent about an hour walking along the falls talking about recent things in their lives. Tristan was not a major part of their conversation, but Renee managed to say some words about him. "What's up with you talking about Tristan so much?" Aurora said with a curious smile.

"He's a good guy. Plus, you never talk about him that much so I might as well start the conversation." Renee said smiling.

Aurora sighed and didn't bother to reply since she knew what it would turn into. The sunset slowly and the stars glittered above. The sky showed no clouds or fog. It was only the big bright moon and millions of stars that sparkled together. They headed to Aurora's car happily and sat inside for a while to admire the view. She didn't know why but Tristan was fresh in her mind. She remembered the week before their anniversary.

He became more withdrawn to her and barely listened when she talked. She didn't know why he had to say he loved her and then left her. Everything seemed to be right between them and then he disappeared, taking every bit of happiness she had. When it was their awaited day, she didn't realize he had already forgotten her. She wasn't the most important thing on his mind anymore. She remembered what he had said the next day when he had arrived at school, and she chased him down to talk to him.

"Give it a rest Aurora. It's always been about you in this relationship. I'm done with you and all of it. Just forget about everything we went through." he had said sharply. For the rest of the year, they didn't talk.

Chapter 14

Days passed and suddenly Aurora only had less than two weeks left. She spent her time with her mom and didn't think about even trying to talk to her dad again. Nothing seemed to change. When she got the chance, she spent time with her friends at the old diner. She didn't open up much about her life and she just listened in on what they wanted to do. Aurora had locked herself in her room more than once to just look back at her old things. She had found her old diary which she started writing in her first year of high school and finished the last entry by the end of senior year.

It was mostly about her inner thoughts which she had never shared with anyone. It went from how much pain she was going through when it came to her parents to how much she liked certain guys. She read the diary over and over again and it showed her how much of a normal girl she proved to be, besides her relationship with her parents. She felt like such a girly girl when she read about how a guy made her feel. After she read her diary, she would throw it under her bed.

When she had about a week and a half left, she got a call from Mike. She was caught off guard and yet she saw it coming at one point. She hesitated to answer but knew she needed to.

"What Mike?" she said harshly.

She heard him chuckle slightly and she winced slightly. The guy had always affected her, and she couldn't deny it.

"Hello to you too dear. I was just making sure you were doing all right." He said playfully.

Aurora held the phone and ran down to the living room where Renee and her mom were. She ran to turn to the TV and placed her phone on the speaker. "Well, I'm doing great. What else do you want?" Aurora seethed into the phone.

He laughed humorlessly and sighed. "I don't want anything, honey. Just wanted to see how you are. It's been a while since we talked." He said simply.

Aurora looked up at Renee and her mom who had smiles plastered on their faces. She smiled back and replied, "Well you know how I am already. If you anything else to say I'm listening." Aurora said knowingly. She heard him sigh through the phone. She smiled and looked at her mom again who smiled sweetly.

"Aurora, can we give us another try? I... I did love you; I think I still do, and I still want to try us out. You didn't give me a chance to see what I did wrong." He said in a whisper.

Renee and Maria were on their toes and practically giggling as they listened in on Aurora's conversation. She felt herself blush "Wow. Look Mike, can we talk about this when I get back to FL? I don't want to have this conversation on the phone." Aurora said with a sigh. She heard his slow breathing through the phone accompanied by a sigh.

"Alright," Mike said roughly.

Aurora ended the call and plopped herself onto the couch. She stared at the phone for some lingering minutes and jumped up suddenly. "Why the hell is he calling now and saying he loves me? I ended it before it could start because he was the one who told me commitment was too exhausting! I even told all the people here that it was because of my commitment issues not his and now he wants to go back in. He has some balls." Aurora said furiously.

Renee tried to think of what to say but nothing came up. Aurora groaned and pulled her hair gently. "What am I going to do? I want to give him a chance, but things are getting too complicated... Maybe I should just end it completely next time I see him." She whispered dully. They sat in a deafening silence and Aurora felt her mind melt into a puddle of nothing.

"Is that really what you want? To just drop him out of your life… forever? I mean the guy called and said he loved you, that doesn't happen often." Maria questioned.

Aurora looked up at her and frowned. "Why not? We weren't right for each other anyway and even if he still loves me, it seemed over before it started." Aurora said bitterly.

Maria shrugged dismissively and looked over at Renee. "Well do what you want. I know you want a steady boyfriend already and I know Mike isn't the best choice for it. The time's ticking on your love clock though." Renee said perceptively.

Aurora groaned silently. "Thanks for the reminder," Aurora said annoyed, and they sat in their cozy living room watching yet again another dramatic soap.

The next day Aurora decided to meet up with Anthony and Roxy. Renee had suggested that Aurora go out and spend time with her old friends. Aurora had wanted to take Renee with her, but Maria had already taken her on a real town tour. She left her house excitedly and drove off to the couple's new condominium. When she reached the condo, she looked at the modern architecture. It looked grand and yet so cozy. She stepped out of her car and glided to the door. She rang the doorbell and waited for an answer. Behind the door, she had heard small laughter and some talking along with rustling. She heard the door open behind her and came face to face with Roxy dressed in only a big towel.

"Uh... Hi?" Aurora said awkwardly. Roxy smiled and laughed uncontrollably as her wet hair dripped water onto her shoulders.

"Don't worry sweetheart you didn't interrupt anything. Ants fully dressed if you look over there near the TV. Come in, would you? I don't want my neighbors thinking crazy thoughts." Roxy said with a gigantic smile.

Aurora laughed uncertainly and walked in. She looked at the living room which, true to Roxy's word, had Anthony fully clothed. Aurora snorted suddenly and Ant turned to see her laughing. "Hey girly looks like Rox said something about her somewhat undressed state." He said grinning.

Aurora smiled wider and walked up to him. As she got closer to him, he pulled her into a tight hug. They heard Roxy clear her throat behind them and they turned to face her clutching her towel tightly. "I'm going to get dressed and we will do something exciting." She said with a bigger grin than Ant.

Aurora watched as Roxy pranced up the stairs and disappeared into a bedroom. She eyed the big couch and plopped her body onto it. She looked over at Ant who was still grinning and sat at the end of the couch near Aurora's feet. He leaned back and sighed heavily. He turned his head and faced Aurora. "I love that girl. She might be the one for me. I sound like such a chick right now huh?" Ant whispered.

Aurora smiled sweetly and propped herself up with her elbow. "No. Not a chick. You're 100% boy uh, man in love. At least you found a girl I approve of. "She whispered back.

Anthony groaned and covered his eyes with his arm. "I think I'm going to propose to her after Jack and Tina get married. You know how I am. I don't want to steal Tina's big day from her. She would punch the daylights outta me." Ant said, rubbing his eyes.

Aurora chuckled and kicked his leg playfully. "Yeah, that's true. I have to admit you're a good guy." She said with a smirk.

"Speaking of love and stuff how are you and Tristan getting along?" he asked cautiously.

Aurora froze a bit and untensed herself. "Good I think but I'm just so confused as to why he did what he did. He just dropped me out of his life like my feelings didn't count and just a week ago he had said he didn't mean to hurt me. I don't understand any of it! If he didn't mean to hurt me, what did he think was going to happen huh? I want to know everything that he didn't tell me." She said loudly.

She felt herself shudder uncomfortably and looked at Anthony's confused state. "He didn't give you a reason. He made a mistake, maybe somewhere down the road it could be fixed but he needs to answer." He said apologetically.

Aurora turned her head away and looked out the nearby window. "I was broken when it happened. I never thought he would have been someone I had to miss." she said solemnly.

She was happy that Ant, Tina, Jack, and Roxy hadn't gone through that pain. All of them had that fairytale ending just around the corner. Anthony smiled faintly and patted Aurora's leg reassuringly. "You'll find someone. Or maybe you already have you just don't know it. That's how it was with Roxy and me." He said quietly.

Aurora didn't know how to answer that. She knew he was just trying to help and yet he was acting like he knew how she felt but no one knew how much she was broken. "And if I don't?" she asked softly. He reached over and held her hand as he gently replied, "You will."

Aurora had spent the rest of her day hanging out with them. It was somewhat weird considering they were a couple now. Aurora had to admit she saw it coming at some point. They had that flirty atmosphere around them. Anthony had told them about some of his students who had been flirting with him and Roxy couldn't help but frown.

"So did you ever flirt back with them?" Roxy fumed jealously.

He snorted slightly and held her closer to him. "Please. You're the only one for me. Plus, the age differences would be so wrong. "He said with a grin.

Roxy blushed and punched him square in the arm. Aurora laughed delicately and watched the couple cuddle together. "You guys are so weird." she said mockingly.

Ant and Roxy turned to her, and both smiled coyly. "Oh, we're weird huh?" Roxy said as moved away from him. Aurora laughed as Roxy stuck her tongue out and walked away slowly toward her kitchen. The doorbell rang and Ant stood up to answer it. Aurora twisted herself slightly to see who was at the door, but he had been blocking the person. Ant moved away and, to Aurora's shock, appeared Tristan. She sat up from her position and quickly busied herself with her phone. She viewed some messages that Mike had sent her asking when she was coming back and so on. She sighed heavily and went back to her curled-up position. She lay on her back and placed her phone above her. Aurora ran her hand through her hair with a deep sigh. Tristan was within a couple of feet away from her and she felt her heart pound mysteriously. Looks like he captured my heart again, Aurora thought with a vague smile. She knew she couldn't let it happen again, but Tristan had always had this effect on her. She felt his presence and knew he didn't know she was there. She closed her eyes tightly and waited till something happened.

She heard deep laughter around her, and she opened her eyes in shock. Tristan had been hovering above her and now he was staring deep into her eyes. His eyes melted into a chocolaty color and his smile fluttered on his lips with amusement.

"Hello there." He whispered sinisterly.

Aurora gulped and blinked in her dazed state. "Hi." She whispered back hesitantly. He stood up straight and still looked at her intently.

"What brings you to the lovebird's nest?" he asked as he walked to an open chair.

Aurora turned her head toward him and stayed in her comfortable position. "I felt like meeting up with them today." She said with a dull smile.

"That's nice," he said with a remarkable smile. She groaned inwardly and turned her head back to the ceiling. They sat in a deafening silence like they had so many times recently and tried to busy themselves with something. Aurora had heard shouting and clatter in the kitchen, and she sat up wearily. She faced Tristan and he looked at her worried. Both of them stood and walked cautiously toward the open kitchen. They stood by the open door and watched as the couple fought.

"Maybe you should tell me what's going on with all of these daily getaways!!" Ant yelled as Roxy walked toward her purse.

"Nowhere should you know about okay I thought you'd have more faith in me than this," Roxy screamed back.

"Well, it's kind of hard to when you don't want to tell me anything. You're supposed to be able to trust me enough to tell me. Since you won't tell me I'm left to think about the possibilities. "He fumed angrily.

Roxy faced him and her face tensed up. "You know what? I don't need to explain anything I do! You should know I'm not that kind of person. If you can't even trust me then just forget about us." Roxy said as she burst into tears and ran out of the kitchen, into the living room, and up the grand stairs. Tristan ran after her and Aurora watched as he knocked on the door and disappeared into the room. Aurora walked into the kitchen and saw Ant gripping onto the marble counter.

Chapter 15

The tension in the air was thick. He had his back to her and Aurora couldn't help but frown at his absurd ways. He was acting too unreasonable.

"I'm guessing you're here to tell me I'm being irrational?" He said stoically.

"Yes, you are, and you should be dumped if you're going to act this way." she said harshly. She saw Ant tense up and cringe.

"It's not my fault that she's been leaving just about every night to go somewhere. You would have done the same thing." He grumbled.

Aurora rolled her eyes. "Yes, you know I would but there's a difference!! I'm a woman and when I ask a guy, I'm used to him shaking off my question. When you ask a girl and you don't know the whole story, you could be reaching conclusions that aren't there, and you know it." She yelled irritated.

He turned to face her fully and an ugly frown marred his face. "So, it's my fault huh?" he whispered. She shrugged and leaned against the door jamb.

She sighed deeply and stared at him. "I never said that. All I said was that you were being super irrational. Now you got to find a way to make it up to her." She replied gently.

They heard the kitchen door behind them open. Tristan came in and walked to the fridge. He opened the door, took out a frozen bag of peas and pulled a stool out to sit. He faced them and there was a giant bruise on his cheek. He placed the bag on his face and groaned. Aurora ran up to him and fussed unconsciously. "Where the heck did you get that from?" She said shocked.

He looked up at her and smiled. "Roxy threw a porcelain figurine at me and nailed me in the face. I curse the day I taught her how to throw." He said as Aurora pushed his hand away to view the bruise.

She winced faintly and placed his hand back onto his face. "Did she tell you anything about what's going on?" Anthony asked curiously.

Tristan turned to face him and replied, "She said she's been leaving every day because your mom was teaching her how to cook. It's a really big deal for her." Anthony looked up confused and his eyes wandered.

"Why does she need to learn? I do all the cooking...Oh... I'm a complete idiot!" Anthony groaned.

Aurora smiled as he finally digested the information. "If I were you, I'd go up there and apologize. I had to take away her car keys to make sure she didn't leave to go somewhere. You know how women get when they're upset." Tristan said as he pulled out a bunch of keys from his pocket. Ant grabbed the keys from Tristan's hand and ran up the stairs quickly. Aurora sighed and Tristan groaned. "That stupid couple gets paranoid so quickly. Little did he know that it was so important for her. The poor girl was babbling about how much of a dumbass he was." Tristan grumbled. Aurora giggled slightly and walked to an open stool.

She kept looking back at Tristan to make sure he was okay and heard him chuckle. "I'm all right Aurora. Don't worry your pretty head too much all right?" He said with a grin as big as his ego.

She snorted and flipped her hair unconsciously. "Tris, you're lucky Roxy can't aim well. If it was me, I would've aimed for that eye of yours." She said with a forged smile, coated with extra sweetness.

He stared at her wide-eyed and shook his head. "I know you would so remind me to never mess with you." He remarked.

"Too bad you already have." She whispered under her breath.

"Excuse me?" he said curiously. Aurora smiled and shook her head.

"Nothing." She replied. He looked at her intently and shrugged her unknown comment off. After the dramatic couple had made up, Aurora sat with Roxy as the boys bonded. "Nice throw their honey." She said with a chuckle.

Roxy smiled as she rubbed her swollen eyes. "I feel so bad. I thought it was Anthony and it turned out to be Tristan. Now he has that bruise on his face." she said shyly.

Aurora laughed and reached out to hold her friend's hand. "It's all right Rox. Considering how he was cracking jokes about it, Tristan is all right with it its better the boy who you've been friends with through thick and thin than, your man." Aurora said kindly.

They got into a steady conversation and noticed the boys had been sneaking looks toward them. "You look amazing Aur. Even Ant can't help to stare." Roxy said with a thoughtful smile.

"There's nothing new about me. I just lost weight and fixed my distractingly curly hair." She said with a grin.

Roxy snorted and leaned toward her. "Here's a secret I think you should know. You've always been amazingly beautiful. You just never realized it." She said with a sparking smile.

Aurora smiled faintly and shrugged. "That's a secret I can't believe." She whispered back.

Roxy laughed and plastered a smile onto her face. Aurora's blue eyes flickered with amusement and her lips pulled into a smirk. "Well Aurora, I guess that's what makes it interesting."

"So, what's new with Aur and you?" Ant said as he took a sip of his drink. Tristan cringed slightly and pinched his arm to stop.

"Nothing changed. We're still in that same awkward zone. I don't think anything will change from this point. I'm leaving in a week and it's not going anywhere. I might as well give up and live the rest of my life alone." He said bitterly.

He already felt so alone he wanted that feeling that Ant and Roxy had every day of their lives. Ant smiled wearily and leaned back on his seat. "Don't think like that. We'll think of something to make it work." he said confidently.

Tristan groaned inwardly and forced a smile. "And what if this plan of yours fails?" Tristan questioned.

Ant smiled deviously and his eyes glittered furiously. "Have I ever failed you, honeybunch?" He said as he reached out his hand and laid it on Tristan's knee.

Tristan was traumatized and pushed Anthony's hand away slowly. "Um, I'm pretty sure you have before." he said as he inched away from him.

Anthony laughed melodiously and wiped away his fake tears. "You never cease to amaze me. I can't believe you can play along so well." He said happily.

Tristan tilted his head back and laughed loudly. When his laughter died out, he turned back toward Anthony. "I hope this plan of yours works." He remarked with a smirk.

Ant looked at him solemnly. "Who said I had a plan? But don't you trust me? I am one of the most helpful people I know. Plus, I'm your wingman. I got this." He said with a cocky grin.

Tristan rolled his eyes and averted his gaze to the women in the kitchen. They sat on the open stools and chatted vigorously about useless womanly things. "Tell me. How is it that Roxy could love a smug man like you? I always thought she went for down-to-earth kind of guys." Tristan said as he shot back a sip of his cool drink.

Ant chuckled darkly and gazed at him coolly. "I'm amazingly handsome and I guess she couldn't resist my charms. I guess it's also the fact that I'm just every girl's prince." He replied as he leaned in toward Tristan.

Tristan smiled and extended his arms above him. "Right now, you sound like Jack. He's the only one who's supposed to be a prince." He commented as Ant frowned.

"I could do it too you know." He pouted childishly.

Tristan smirked and closed his eyes. He couldn't help but think of how much this guy had changed from their youth. Once long ago, Tristan had been extremely jealous of this man. Aurora had always bragged about how Ant could do this and that before they had dated. Aurora was completely smitten by him and was nonstop asking Tristan questions about him, even if the both of them lived next to each other. Within time, Tristan had learned how to control his feelings, and he wooed Aurora into his life. He was such an egotistical person though and he lost the one person he needed most.

"Ant, am I a shallow person?" He asked. Ant thought for a moment and shook his head.

"Nothing near it my friend." He replied with a genuine smile. Tristan nodded and averted his mind to another topic.

As the day drew on, Aurora helped Anthony cook dinner. Roxy had wanted to help but Ant had told her to keep Tristan company. Aurora had thought this would have sparked the fuel between them, but it hadn't. She just complied stubbornly and pranced off into the living room quickly.

Roxy walked up to Tristan silently and plopped herself next to him on the couch. "So, Tris, have you made a move on Aurora yet?" she asked as she leaned against his slouching position. Tristan groaned unconsciously and looked down at her.

"You know, I regret telling you about how I felt about her." He said with a deep frown. She lifted her arm around Tristan's waist and pulled him into an awkward hug.

"Please. It's good you told me in the first place or else you would've burst from not telling anyone." she said as she squeezed him tight. He wiggled out of her grasp, but her arms had locked around him. She laughed sweetly and gripped him tighter. "Stop moving!! I'm trying to hug my pal here!" She said as he wriggled away.

Tristan stood up and jumped behind the couch. "You won't be able to catch me!!" he said as he bolted towards the kitchen.

"Tristan Alvarez, you narcissistic moron don't run away from me!! You know I can hurt you! That big bruise on your face proves it. All I want is a stupid hug!" She yelled as she dashed toward him.

"I'm so scared!" He mocked as he jogged away from her. Tristan ran into the kitchen and grabbed Ant to stand in front of him as she entered the kitchen. Tristan watched as Roxy crossed her arms in front of her and pouted. She started crying and Tristan felt Ant tense up in front of him.

"C'mon man, she's playing us. You know she's good at faking her tears. Don't you dare move?" He whispered to Ant. Roxy inched closer to them and Tristan stepped back, pulling Ant with him.

"Anthony, he's being a dummy," Roxy whined dramatically. She advanced closer and Tristan backed up, only to hit a wall. Roxy walked up to Tristan's man shield and kissed him smack on the lips. Ant lowered his head toward her and kissed her back happily. Before he knew it, Tristan had lost Ant to her, and he was left to think of another solution. After Roxy had let go of Ant, she grinned at Tristan mischievously and charged toward him for a hug. This time she had prevailed and held him in a death grip. "I gotcha! So, what do I win?" she said with a glitter of amusement plastered on her face. They walked back to the living room slowly with Roxy still gripping onto him. Tristan looked down at her and sighed in defeat.

"Who said you win anything?" He said smiling.

Roxy grinned and let go of him. "I did so I know what I want from you," Roxy said with a bigger grin.

Tristan gulped visibly and hung his head. "Oh, please share." He said with forged enthusiasm.

She smiled sinisterly and whispered it into his ear. "You are going to plan something with Aurora whether you like it or not. Got it?" He felt his heart flutter wildly and watched as Roxy stood in front of him with her hands on her hips. Would he be able to be with Aurora for an entire day without spilling his secret? He had done it before but if it was just the two of them it seemed impossible.

Before he was able to answer, he heard Aurora laugh overwhelmingly. He heard mini shrieks coming from her in the kitchen and listened to them intently.

"She has such a pretty laugh." He said instinctively.

Roxy grinned at him happily and patted his shoulder lightly. "Think of it as me doing you the biggest favor of your life. This is what will seal the deal between you and her. This is what's going to show what will happen to both of you. I just want you to be happy." Roxy whispered slowly.

"That's absolutely true. I'll think of something." He said with a faint smile. Within minutes, they both had been called by Ant and they headed to the dining room.

They ate dinner with a lively conversation about Anthony's job and Tristan stayed silent as he contemplated what he was going to do. It was such a troublesome task. He played with his food involuntarily. He knew Aurora's likes and dislikes when they were younger and hoped her preferences hadn't changed. Her competitive lifestyle helped her throughout her life. Tristan had tried beating her at her competitiveness, but he fell short. It was too tiring for him. He remembered also how much she had been interested in music. Once she had wanted to learn how to play piano but was already too busy with her schedule. She had been balancing so many things and she had tried to make sure she spent some time with her friends every day besides school. He had to think…

Her smiles from that night had been sealed into the depths of his brain and heart. He chuckled silently and looked up from his plate of food in front of him. Silence enwrapped his ears, and he looked up at the worried faces of his friends.

"Tris, are you alright?" Roxy asked with a worried look.

He smiled at her distraughtly and nodded slowly. "Never better." He whispered lightly. The night went on and as soon as it had started, the day had ended.

Chapter 16

When Aurora woke up, the sun had barely peeked past the window. She groaned lazily as she thought about tomorrow being her last day here. She promised herself that she would still be in touch with the people here she had tended to forget about. Her relationship with her mom was still on shaky ground but Aurora knew she had forgiven her mom for all her previous discomforts. Her dad was unreachable, and she felt as if she didn't want to bother talking to him. And then there was Tristan. She knew she still needed to talk to him about the past and she planned to do it while she was still here. She never knew it would be this hard to talk to him. When they were younger, he was always reachable. Things changed though.

With caution, she walked out of her room and almost tripped over Renee's sleeping body.

"Renee?" Aurora said loudly while tapping the woman with her foot. Renee stirred slowly and groaned uncomfortably.

"Aurora you better have a good reason for last night. I spent the damn night on this stupid floor." Renee said with a frown.

Aurora lifted her and they walked into her room. Renee plopped herself onto Aurora's bed and cuddled with a tattered monkey. "You got some things to share so start already," Renee said happily.

Aurora rolled her eyes and groaned. "We're leaving the day after tomorrow. There's a problem at the restaurant." Aurora said monotonously.

"What!? Why?? We have to stay longer! They can't decide when your vacation ends!" Renee wailed throwing the monkey onto a pillow.

Aurora paced around the room and faced the wall. "Well, I have to but if you want to you can stay. You rented that car from here, right? Well, I need to take a plane ride since I have a meeting the day I go back. I want you to take my car and drive it back to FL for me." Aurora said in a business-like tone.

Renee couldn't believe it. Aurora was acting so cold, and she was treating her like a secretary, instead of her best friend. Maybe she had wanted to stay here for her intended time but hadn't wanted to say so. "Alright, I'll do that BOSS," Renee said with an emphasis on the boss as she walked out of the room. Aurora groaned and slapped her forehead. She ran to her suitcases and picked out her clothes for the day. After dressing she ran through her house and out the door, leaving Renee in an upset mood.

This is so stupid. What am I thinking? Aurora thought as she drove up to a small, cozy house. She parked her car on the curb and sat in the car for a couple of minutes. When she built up her confidence, she exited the car and walked towards the door. I hope I have the right house, she thought panicking. She rang the doorbell slowly and heard unraveling shouts inside the house. Her heartbeat quickened as she stood for a lingering minute outside the house. The door was opened by a teenage boy who had excruciatingly beautiful green eyes and was also holding a water bottle. The boy gazed at her with wide eyes and his mouth gaped open and Aurora smiled. He looked around sixteen yet had a mature essence around him.

"Hey, Manny remember me?" Aurora said with a flirty smile.

Manny's eyes opened wide, and he dropped his water bottle. "No, but hell I wish I did. Summer camp? Football games? Where have you seen me before I can't believe I overlooked you. "He asked incredulously.

He motioned Aurora into the warm house that smelled like sugar and cinnamon. Aurora giggled and replied, "It's a secret." She heard a woman's voice in the next room and headed closer to them. Mrs. Alvarez walked in with a very shocked face. Her mahogany brown hair was immaculately tied in a ponytail and her skin glowed.

"Mom, I think you have a visitor, an extremely beautiful visitor." he said, whispering the last part.

Aurora laughed and looked back at Mrs. Alvarez. "Hello, Mrs. Alvarez. How are you?" She said with a sweet smile.

Mrs. Alvarez ran to Aurora and engulfed her in a hug. "Aurora Mathews!! I can't believe you're here! This is amazing! You look amazing! Manny, don't you remember her?" She said happily.

Mrs. Alvarez smiled and ran off to the kitchen. Manny looked back at Aurora and his eyes widened again. Shock was written all over his face. "No. You can't be Aurora Mathews. You're too gorgeous, not that Aur wasn't gorgeous, but you're incredibly sexy." He said disbelievingly.

Aurora laughed and walked over to Manny who was almost taller than her. "Oh, it's me alright Manny." She said with a smirk. He blinked at her and his eyes brightened.

"Wow. How old are you?" he asked with a smile. She turned away from him and looked over her shoulder.

"Too old for you." She said as she walked away from him, his mouth still open.

She entered the kitchen and saw Mr. Alvarez reading the newspaper. As her heels clicked onto the wood floor, he lowered the paper and looked up at her. He stared at her disbelievingly and smiled warmly.

"Aurora come here and give this old man a hug." He said with a chuckle. Aurora walked up to him, hugged him tightly, and sat beside him. "So, Aurora what brings you to our humble home?"

She shrugged and looked at Manny in the living room. "I haven't seen you all in a while and I'm leaving soon so I might as well quickly visit and say hello. Anyway, where is Tristan? I was supposed to meet him here." She said, lying about the last part. "Oh well, Tristan's in his room. Are you all right with talking with him? You haven't seen or talked to each other in so many years. Do you want me to go with you?" Mrs. Alvarez said wearily.

Aurora laughed and shook her head. "There's no need to. He hasn't told you about seeing me more than once? When I got here a couple of weeks ago, he saw me and then the reunion. Besides that, there have been other times. We're on okay terms now." Aurora said with a grin.

The couple looked at each other and rolled their eyes. "Then do you know why he has that gigantic bruise on his face?" Mr. Alvarez asked with a smug smile.

"Yeah, I do but I promise it wasn't me. If I were going to hurt him it would have been more severe." She said with a mischievous grin.

The couple smiled and sent Aurora up to their oldest child's room. She walked unsteadily toward Tristan's room, and she felt herself tense up. So many memories were made here. Those little stolen kisses were breathtaking, nevertheless. They shared many of them and it wasn't just in one room of this house. She walked up to the door of his room and knocked. Behind the door, she heard rustling and Tristan grumbling to himself. The door pulled open, and he looked at her surprised. His hair was disheveled and added a flare to him. He was in casual jeans and a green long-sleeved shirt which clung to his sculpted body and made him look devilishly handsome. Aurora thought there was something wrong with how she described him, but it was all too true.

"Hey, Tris." She said nervously.

He grinned and motioned her into his room. Just as it was before, his room was immaculately clean and organized. It was unusual for a boy to be as such, but Tristan had ambitious standards. Maybe he was meant to be a doctor for those reasons. She sat on his comfy bed, and he sat across from her in his computer chair. The air wasn't as tense as it was the first time. Now it felt as if it were old times. "So, Aurora, what brings you to my humble home?" he asked with a steady smile.

Before she was able to respond the door opened and Manny came in. He sat next to Aurora and stared at her strongly, his green eyes glittering.

"Um Manny, why are you staring at me like that?" She said as she shifted and looked over at Tristan. Manny didn't say anything, so Tristan threw a tennis ball at him, and he caught it without looking.

"I'm just seeing if it's Aurora. You all can lie to me all you want but I need proof that it's you. I mean seriously, when did you learn how to flirt back? You sucked at that." He said as he ogled at her.

She laughed flirtatiously and batted her long eyelashes. "Is that so? I always thought I was rather good at it." She said with a pout.

Manny's mouth gaped open again and he shook his head briskly. Tristan laughed and watched as the pushy teen looked at her in awe. "Man, it is her. I promise you can even ask her any question about her, and she'd know." Tristan said with a smug smile.

Manny looked back at her and squinted hard. "Fine, what is my favorite place to be at?" he said arrogantly.

Tristan and Manny were siblings. They had that same look to them and the same annoying demeanors. It was quite mind-boggling for her, and she felt immensely weird when she thought of the similarities. The only difference was Manny's bright green eyes. Aurora had always thought he had amazing eyes. She still did. That was how she remembered his favorite place.

"Your favorite place is the forest in my backyard because I once told you the lush green reminded me of your eyes." She spoke.

Manny blinked and jumped out of the bed with a cheer. "I can't believe it's you!" He said as he pulled her into a tight hug. Aurora giggled and lifted her arm to pat him on the head lightly. He pulled her at arm's length and gazed into her eyes. "You still owe me that car you promised when I was 8." He said in a serious tone.

She looked up at him and burst into laughter. She rolled on Tristan's bed, dying with laughter and trying to catch her breath, to no avail. As she caught her breath she stood up and slapped him on the shoulder.

"Keep dreaming kiddo. My car is forever off-limits to you." She said with a smile. Manny smiled and Aurora walked away down the stairs. He plopped onto Tristan's bed and smiled wide.

"How could you have ever let that get out of your grip? She's dynamite man." He said while pointing at Aurora as she descended the stairs.

Tristan frowned at him and turned to face his computer. Manny raised his hands in defeat and sat up. "Do you think she'd go on a date with me?" he said with a vague smile.

Tristan spun in his chair and looked at his younger brother. "Yeah, I bet she would. That is if you don't tell her, it's a date." Tristan said with a charming smile. He turned back to his computer and Manny threw a pillow at him.

Tristan burst into laughter and Manny responded to his comment. "I look exactly like you except for my striking green eyes, as she said they were before," Manny said with an overconfident smile.

Tristan rolled his eyes and walked out of his room and down the stairs. He heard Aurora and his parents laughing loudly. The way he had hurt her before flashed into his mind and he couldn't help but feel completely guilty. He knew her parents were already on the brink of a divorce, yet he hadn't tried to stay with her to keep her strong. He knew it was only him who would've helped her out. If he hadn't screwed up, then there might have been a chance that she would have stuck around in his life. Why had he broken up with her when she needed him the most? He still didn't know an exact answer, but he knew that the questions were coming.

Chapter 17

Aurora had spent the day with Tristan's family, she needed to talk to him alone but every time she tried, they were interrupted by a family member. She knew his family was trying to fill in every moment they had with each other to be less tense, but little did they know she needed this. She needed to talk to him and let this unsettling past they had disappear. She wanted him back in her life even if she had to settle as friends. She didn't know what else she wanted from it.

"Aurora? You still alive?" Tristan said as he tapped her bare shoulder.

Aurora flinched and he winced too. "I'm here don't worry. I was just thinking about something." She said as he pulled his hand back.

He looked away from her and listened as his parents droned on about their recent adventures. "What are you thinking about?" He said in a whisper.

Aurora shivered lightly and smiled. "Nothing you need to know about." She said in a singsong whisper.

Tristan smiled and sat next to her on the dull living room couch. "Look dear. No need to get all sassy with me." He said with a smile.

She eyed his smile and felt her heart pound ungracefully. This needed to happen before her heart took over and she decided now was the time. She groaned and stood up. "You, me, in your room, now," Aurora said as she pointed up the stairs.

Tristan looked up at her in disbelief and walked toward the stairs with a smile. His family stared at their display, and she felt a blush creep up in her body. "That was rather forward of you. You know how much my parents love gossip." Tristan whispered as he walked close behind her. They ran up the stairs and into his room, which had suddenly become disorganized. They both got in and she shut the door behind her. She turned to face Tristan and braced herself against the door. ' Crap, this is awkward, she thought shakily. "So, what was your purpose for this little get-together?" he asked with a raised eyebrow.

She wiggled in her position and played with the doorknob. "Um, I uh actually have no idea?" She said as confusion filled her thoughts.

Tristan chuckled and gave her a knowing look. He stood up from his position on a chair and walked towards her. He stopped in front of her barely far enough to feel her anxiety. "Is that so?" he said with a dark chuckle. His hand came up to her arm and his fingers dragged along her bare arm. She felt the hair on her arms stand and she shivered unconsciously. She couldn't respond to his utterly unexpected actions. Her body was betraying her. She wasn't supposed to be enjoying his closeness. She felt the warmth from his body emanating from her.

As usual, his masculine scent was too sinful, and Aurora felt as if it was attracting her towards him more. It was too unfair for her. His hand stopped at her mid-shoulder, and he propped his arms on the wall behind her. Her mouth went dry, and she turned her head to face away from him. His hands came to her face and tilted her head to his face. He smiled deviously and placed his hand on her shoulder. "You sure you don't have a reason?" He whispered.

The warmth of his breath triggered memories, and she couldn't help but blush uncontrollably. Her breaths became labored and fast. What was he doing to her? All her instincts revolved around him at that moment. His smell, the way he looked, the feel of his soft hand on his shoulder. Everything… He was everywhere and everything on her mind at the moment. If it was love or lust she didn't care. One thing was on her mind. She needed to set it straight. She needed to clear the air between them. She prayed to God that this wasn't the end.

"We need to talk Tris. That's why I'm here." Tristan's eyes widened and he backed away from her winded body. He sighed and rubbed his face vigorously. He knew this was going to happen at some point, yet it was so unexpected. He felt relief and panic at the same time. Her blunt response was all he needed to understand her mind. She was practically surrendering to his touch moments ago. He didn't have an explanation worth her time and thought. She must have worried about the subject for a long time, but he felt as if he was going to disappoint her more than he already had. "Look Aur. I can't give you an exact reason for that mistake. I know I screwed up, but I don't know why I did it. That's all I can say and truthfully, I don't know how to make it up to you. I guess it was because I was scared." He said casually.

She felt her heart pound and threatened to break yet again. "What do you mean you don't know why?! Are you kidding me, Tristan? To think after all these years, you would have thought that through and be ready to give me an answer! Don't you think that I was heartbroken by that? My parents were getting worse as a couple, and I thought you were the one who'd be able to be there for me. Instead, you were just another face in the crowd who watched as I went through it all alone. Didn't you even think about me in this?" She shrieked.

He scowled and paced around the room. "I'm telling you the truth alright. Trust me just this once! I knew you were going through all of this and I wasn't thinking about past the fact that I couldn't be with you. I wanted to be with you, but everything seemed to be in the way. College was right around the corner, and I had my dream ahead of me. I didn't know what to do. I guess I chose what I wanted after you since I knew at one point you'd hurt me in the end. Turns out I screwed up incredibly and hurt my only chance at happiness with you. So don't say you were the only one who went through some pain, all right?" he said firmly.

She gasped and clutched onto the wall behind her. "If you're just saying all of this to make me buy it, save it you already hurt me once I don't know why you should do it again." She whispered.

Tristan pulled her to him, and he held her shoulders. "Trust me on this, please. Quit being stubborn and listen to me, I wouldn't have said it all if I were telling you my true feelings. You should know me better than that!" he said pleadingly.

She pulled away from him and crossed her arms. "Fine… Let's forget about it. I know I'm dying too. That is, about everything." She said as she walked out of the room. "Aurora wait a second, will you?" Tristan said as he chased her down the stairs. She was already getting her stuff together and Tristan reached out for her arm. He gripped her arm and she didn't turn to face him. "Look. I know you wanted this to work out better and be less dramatic so try to make me understand what you want me to since I don't know." he said calmly.

She closed her eyes and sighed through suddenly tear-filled eyes. "It's all right now Tristan. We don't have problems with each other now and I guess that's how we should leave it. We said everything we needed to, right? "She replied as she tugged her arm from him. She bid his family goodbye quickly and she stormed out of the house just like she had entered.

Chapter 18

Aurora felt herself almost collapse as she entered her car. Her emotions had finally clashed, and she felt it was all too hard to handle. She drove away and headed to her house. As she neared the house she had changed her mind. This home was not an option at the moment. She groaned and her tears spilled once again. She didn't know what to do. Her head was bursting in pain, and she felt her eyes sting. She decided to leave tomorrow. She couldn't take it anymore. She thought it was just a problem with her dad but now Tristan was an addition.

She parked in front of the house and sat in the car, staring at the house. This was practically her last day and yet she didn't think she'd last. Her mind was overflowing with mixed emotions, and she didn't know what she wanted to happen. When it came to these things, she was always prepared. Now it felt as if she had been blindsided. She didn't want to fall off the face of her friend's world and yet she knew she had to. She couldn't say goodbye again. It was too late. Since Renee was still there, they'd be able to talk to her and ask about Aurora's whereabouts if she needed them to. She would be back for Tina and Jack's wedding next month. She had made up her mind but at that moment she couldn't deal with this. She needed a drink, or three.

She raced her car into the slowly slumbering town and viewed the main street for a local bar. She took note of Johnny's Bar which was at a busy corner. She parked her car and exited quickly. She briskly walked into the bar. When she walked in, the smell of smoke plagued her instincts. She heard low mumbling from various parts of the bar and glasses clinking lightly. She walked towards the counter and sat on an open stool. Familiar faces watched her, and their gazes lingered a little more than once. The bartender turned to her, and it turned out to be Mark Webber. He turned to her and his dark eyes sparkled. His hair looked disheveled and yet put a dangerous edge to him.

"I didn't think I'd see you here." He chuckled as he gripped the glass counter.

Aurora shrugged and leaned against her arm. "That's interesting. I didn't think I'd see you here either." She said with a dull smile. Mark eyed her suspiciously and looked at her seriously.

"Something happen? Another breakup with a cheating boyfriend? Maybe you came here to accept the date that I offered you?" He said with a sweet smile.

Aurora laughed lightly and beamed at him. "No boyfriend cheating on me and sadly I can't accept your date. I leave tomorrow and there are still a lot of things I left undone. It's just the same old stuff you know, just Tristan Alvarez and my parents. Well, more of my dad than my mom." She said with a sigh.

Mark nodded and sighed as well. "Well, the whole class thought you and Tristan were meant to be. Maybe you are and you just have to go through that last hurdle before it works out completely. Right now, I think you could use a drink. What do you prefer?" Mark said as he waved to the shelves of liquor.

"Malibu Bay breeze with a tequila shot, please." She said with a vague smile. He smiled and rushed away. She sat and her thoughts floated around. Mark's comment about Tristan and her floated around in her mind. Were they meant to be? She didn't think so but inside her, there was a spark of contentment that he had said so. She heard a glass clink onto the counter in front of her and she was pulled back to reality. Mark placed the sweet-smelling drink in front of her and eyed her carefully.

"I knew you drank girly drinks like that. Can't hold your alcohol?" he said with a teasing smile. She rolled her eyes and took a sip of her drink.

"Mark, what do you mean by Tristan, and I being meant for each other?" she asked with a confused look.

He sighed and shook his head. "You don't know? I thought you would know since you're a girl and all that romance crap just flows out of you. I guess it's because you all are so uncoordinatedly perfect for each other. It's hard to explain but all I can say is that both of you will get through it." He said with a satisfied smile.

Another customer walked up to the counter and Mark left her for lingering minutes. Her mind was set on Tristan and all the possibilities, but it was hopeless. She almost forgot it was him who broke it off. She had so many hopes and dreams for both of them, but she knew it wasn't only up to her. Tristan didn't want her. Renee had also told her he had a girlfriend. Why had she thought it was going to work the way she had wanted? She was being delusional and too much of a dreamer. It was a dangerous combo, but she couldn't help it. She promised herself to give up and she knew it would be worth it in the end when she was done with the emotional pain. She picked up her drink and chugged it without thinking. She felt the wooziness she had intended to feel after three or four shots kicked in. She felt her body become less tense. She called Mark over and within moments she had four more drinks.

Tristan had been worried. Mark Webber had called him unexpectedly and told him to get Aurora from Johnny's Bar. He noticed whenever something had happened to Aurora while she was here, he was called. He didn't know what had happened to her and Mark himself hadn't added too much detail. It was already eleven o'clock at night and he was already ready for bed. He had pulled on the quickest things he was able to find, which were jeans and a T-shirt. He hadn't bothered to find a jacket since it had been an unusually warm winter night. He stopped by Manny's room to tell him he wasn't going to be back and knew his words would have made Manny do something stupid. He ran to his car in the garage and left as quickly as he could. His drive through town was uneventful. His mind was drifting towards Aurora and all the possibilities of what had happened to her. He tried to stay as optimistic as he was able to, but he couldn't.

That was the downside of being a doctor. He had faced death so many times when it came to his job that he had wondered why he wasn't emotionally scarred. He finally reached the busy bar and noticed Aurora's car parked on the side. He parked quickly and ran into the bar. He looked everywhere for Aurora, but he couldn't see her. He saw Mark behind the counter and remembered that he was working there. Mark had seen him too and motioned Tristan toward him with a worried expression. He finally saw Aurora slumped onto the counter and sitting on a stool. He saw her smiling at Mark and mumbling useless nothings to him. Of course, she was drunk. Tristan walked toward her, and he sat next to her on a different stool. He had never seen her drunk before. She had left before the drinking legality, and he didn't expect her to even look as ditzy as she was.

He had to admit, it was funnier than he thought it was going to be. She looked over at him with a squint and propped herself up with her arm. She looked at him again and frowned before clumsily dropping her arm and her head. She giggled unconsciously and turned back to Tristan. "G go a-away." she said with a hiccup. He watched as she stood from her stool and almost tripped. Before she fell, he jumped from his seat and caught her. She wriggled in his arms and mumbled incoherently.

"You're drunk Aurora. You might hurt yourself." he said sternly.

She pulled free from him and stood up shakily. Her legs buckled and she almost fell, but luckily, she grabbed onto him, and he caught her. She giggled again and slumped back onto an open stool. Mark walked to them and gave Tristan a sympathetic look.

"She had one too many. She is such a lightweight." He said with a good-natured snort.

She frowned and pursed her lips. "I'm not a-a light w-weight." She stuttered. Tristan shook his head and pulled her out of her seat. He carried her over his shoulder, and she shrieked.

She moved around briskly, and he became worried that she would fall from his grip. She hit him back with small slaps and protests. When they got out of the bar he walked, with her on his shoulder, toward his car. Her small disputes wore out and she lay on his shoulder silently. When they got to his car, he placed her in the back seat, so she was able to lie down if she wanted to. Before he shut the door, she reached out and grabbed his wrist. Her grip tightened around him, and she smiled.

"You look like someone I know." she said quietly between hiccups.

Tristan smiled faintly. "Is that good or bad?" He said teasingly.

She giggled dizzily and released her grip. He pulled his arm away and watched as Aurora swayed slowly. "Good. No, bad. Well, both." she said with confusion written all over her face.

Tristan thought she was finally snapping out of her daze, but she wasn't since her voice was still slurred and her giggling was too unlike her. It seemed as though she got worse as the time ticked by. He shut the door and entered the driver's seat.

He drove away from the bar and toward his parents' house. The whole drive Aurora had mumbled about random things, and he couldn't help but laugh more than once because of her comments. When he had reached his parents' house, he looked into the driveway to see his parents' car gone. Instead, there was a Gray Honda parked in the spot. Tristan stepped out of his car and went to retrieve Aurora, who had sobered up quite a bit. He carried her wedding style toward the door and knocked on it loudly. He heard Manny laughing behind the door and as he opened it, his face fell.

"I thought you said you weren't going to come back here." he said hastily. Manny's gaze fell to Aurora's wriggling body, and she smiled up at him.

"Hey, Manny-bear." She said with yet another giggle.

He looked up at Tristan and smiled. "Never thought I'd see her drunk." Tristan walked toward the living room to set Aurora on the couch but there were a bunch of teenagers already there. The two girls looked more conservative than any teen girls he had seen lately.

Two other boys were sitting as well and held that jock-like personality. Tristan stood in front of them and their eyes lingered on him.

"Uh hey, you guys. I'm Manny's brother, Tristan." He said kindly.

Aurora slapped him on the shoulder, and he looked down at her. She frowned at him and wriggled out of his grasp.

"I can walk now." she said stoically. She stood up shakily and flattened her skirt as well as her top. Tristan reached out and grabbed her waist to make sure she wasn't going to fall. She looked back at him with a dirty look and his hand gripped onto hers. Manny walked in and watched as the tense air between Aurora and Tristan affected his friends on the nearby couch.

"Don't mind them; they've always been this irrational." He said as his friends eyed the couple, confused. Aurora snatched her hand away from him and wobbled toward Manny. Manny watched as his guy friends eyed Aurora intensely. He felt that protectiveness he had always had for her kick in, and he threw them both a dirty look.

"Manny, your brother's being mean," Aurora said with a frown. Tristan smiled at this display and crossed his arms.

The two girls on the couch watched him intently and he felt their strong gazes. Manny chuckled lightly and pulled her in for a hug. Her scent was as it always was vanilla and a hint of sweet peas. Now she had a small clue of apples.

"Aurora you never stop amazing me." He said loudly. He felt her shiver in his arms and thought her legs were going to give way. As he let go of her, Tristan stepped in and took hold of her.

"I'm going to take her for a while Manny. You better stay out of trouble since Mom and Dad will be back soon." He said as he took hold of Aurora. Luckily, she hadn't fought back when he pulled her away from the crowd. As they left, Manny's friends were in a frenzy. They were dumbstruck by the two people they had just met. Manny looked as the hopeful duo walked away up the stairs. Both of them should have just confessed to loving the other. Manny had always hoped Aurora would come back and his naïve brother would realize how perfect she was for him. He knew it was more complicated than that. Her heart was extremely fragile, and his brother was meant to be the guy to fix it since he had already broken it in the first place.

Chapter 19

Tristan practically dragged her to his room since her legs kept giving way. When they had entered the confinement of his room, she fell onto his bed unceremoniously. She mumbled incoherent words and looked up at him confused.

"I need a hug." She slurred.

He walked over to her slowly and hugged her tightly. She looked up at him and kissed him soundly on the lips. He opened his eyes in shock and groaned silently against her lips. She was softer than he remembered. His heart soared and he felt heaven finally knock on his door within a minute. He kissed her back fiercely and she moaned against him. He didn't know what was happening between them. He was on fire with passion he remembered feeling many times before with her. She pulled away quickly and fell back against a pillow. As soon as her head hit his pillow, she fell into a deep sleep. He paced around his room with a small smile and watched as she writhed around on the bed. He heard her small snores and couldn't help but laugh.

Manny was right. How could he have ever let her out of his life? It was a stupid mistake. That brother of his had some good qualities, besides gaining his good looks from him. He was trying to make it better, but her spirited ways always got the better of their conversations. She knew how to make conversation about all his faults. She knew how to make herself the victim of his screw-ups. Whether it was how her job changed her or her life itself, he didn't like it at all. She wasn't exactly the girl he had remembered loving once long ago. And then there was that kiss. It was better than he remembered. He started to think of all the other men who had kissed her and frowned knowing he was being irrational. In the morning, he knew she wouldn't have known what had happened, but he knew he would remember always. Before he forgot, he called Renee to tell her about Aurora's whereabouts.

"Hello?" he heard over the phone.

"Sounds like I woke you up. Sorry chickee." Tristan said lightly.

He heard Renee laugh sleepily. "It's all right. Do you know where Aurora is? I've tried calling her all day and she hasn't called back. I'm worried." she said groggily.

"She's with me. She was at a bar and now she's drunk, so I brought her back to my house. I bet she'll tell you the whole story when she sobers up if she remembers." He said with a chuckle.

"Thank God. I was really worried about her. She barely gets drunk. It's only after a bad incident or a break-up. Maybe this time she just couldn't take it." She said with a sigh.

Tristan messed with his hair and groaned. "Alright well, I'll let her stay here and, in the morning, I'll help her get her car. I'll crash in my brother's room since she's already deep asleep and last I checked she was a heavy sleeper." He said as he looked over at her. He heard Renee laugh lightly.

"Yeah, she is. And I'm quite sure she snores loudly too." She said sympathetically. Tristan held his phone near Aurora, and she snored deafeningly into it. He heard Renee laugh and Aurora rolled over.

"Yeah, she does night Renee." he said as he hung up the phone. He tossed his phone onto the bedside table and sat at the foot of the bed. He looked over at Aurora who just happened to be smiling. She must be having a good dream, he thought with a smile, must be about that kiss. She had looked so serene and happy. He wished that he would have been able to see that look on her face when she was awake. Sleep was on his mind but before that was able to happen, he needed to make sure the teens downstairs weren't breaking laws. He walked out of the room and shut the door slowly.

Laughter spread throughout the halls and Tristan walked to the origin in the living room. He walked down the stairs and noted one of the girls giving Manny a shy look. He smiled as a memory invaded his thoughts. The girl reminded him of Aurora when she was younger. Even if she didn't know, he had always caught her steady smiles and wanting looks. Now this girl was directly looking at Manny as he talked with wanting eyes. Tristan walked into the room and their conversation wore out. He knew what they were thinking. He was a teenager once too and he remembered how his friends and he reacted when an adult walked in.

"Don't mind me. I just want to be in on the teen gossip. It'll make me feel younger." He said as he plopped onto the couch next to the girl who seemed to like Manny.

Manny's gaze tightened on Tristan as he placed his arm behind the girl, without touching her. They got into a steady conversation about their senior year. Tristan contributed to the talk and told them about his experiences. He even added things about Aurora and how he broke her heart. The guys stared at him intently and promised not to make that mistake with a girl. The girls had given him looks of disdain, but he had shrugged them off. Tristan heard more about his brother's lifestyle since he hadn't talked to him about it in a while. It sounded like he had fun.

Time passed quickly and it turned out to be midnight already. The group of teens had left, and Tristan was exhausted. That day was tiring and surprisingly it revolved around Aurora. Manny had run to his room and passed out quicker than Tristan expected. Tristan walked to his room and sat on his chair. He turned to face Aurora and heard her soft snores. Even if she were a closed book, he knew she would have been easy to fix within time. His eyes closed unconsciously and within minutes, he was asleep with a smile just as she was.

Chapter 20

When Aurora woke up, she had a pounding headache. She didn't remember the night before. The last thing she remembered was entering Johnny's and talking to Mark. Then the night was a blur. She sat up and looked around the room. It was a familiar room but she couldn't put her finger on it. She saw Tristan slumped on his computer chair fast asleep. She groaned as a sharp pain spread throughout her head. Her lips tingled as she tapped them and looked over the mirror on her side. She looked as if she had run through a jungle. Her eyes were harshly tired-looking, and her lips were swollen as if she had been kissed too furiously. Not that she had been kissed in a while. Maybe it had to do with the hangover. She saw Tristan stir and he opened his eyes suddenly.

His eyes were a dull color and as he yawned, they sparkled with gold. He looked at her with a smile and stood up. She watched as he stretched, and she only noticed how tall he was. He was probably nearing six foot. Tall, dark, and handsome; this man was incredible.

"Why am I here?" She said with a groan.

Tristan chuckled and looked down at her. "You had a fun night out and I swooped in to pull you out of the ditch you dug for yourself. In other words, last night you were drunk." He said kindly.

She rolled her eyes and flopped back. "No wonder I feel crappy. And why am I here? You didn't specify that." She said as she looked up at the ceiling.

"I didn't want to bring you home since it was late. You're interesting when you're drunk. I'm used to you being so stoic and serious. It was nice seeing you lay back and ditzy. Plus, you mumbled more than one stupid thing, and it was pretty funny." He said with a grin.

Aurora blushed and sat up to face him. "Well, I barely get drunk. Ask Renee." she said quietly.

He chuckled and stretched with a yawn. He held his hand out to her and smiled. "A thanks Tristan would do. Let's get some breakfast, shall we?" He said with a small bow. She hesitated to take his hand but did so anyway. Warmth flooded her being and she couldn't help but smile shyly. He guided her down the stairs and into the living room which only contained Manny. He smiled knowingly as he saw the duo walk into the kitchen.

Tristan pulled out a chair for her and she blushed as she took it. The brothers had then made her breakfast, which had been a ritual for them. Aurora looked around the cozy kitchen and looked at the family pictures on the wall. There was one of the three siblings. Aurora had pondered silently about where Angie had gone. Angie was the middle child and the only girl, to Mrs. Alvarez's inconvenience. She had the same dazzling dark eyes as Tristan, and she was amazingly pretty. She was practically Aurora's sister and luckily, she had chewed Tristan out when they had broken up. Angie had blamed everything on Tristan and insisted that he had screwed up entirely.

"So, you guys, what's Ang up to these days?" she said as she rubbed her head.

Manny smiled up at her and rolled his eyes. "College. I think she's dating that guy, Sam or Eddie. I never could keep up with her latest flings. She's studying to be a nurse. You know one of those nurses for newborn babies." Manny said with a confident smile.

Aurora smiled. It was perfect for her lifestyle and personality. "That's nice." She said as Manny placed a plate in front of her. She eyed the plate wearily. "I think this is too much." She said as she poked at her food with her fork. The brothers crossed their arms in front of themselves and frowned.

"Is that a nicer way for you to say you don't want to eat the food we cooked for you? I make no promises that we did something to it." Tristan said with a smile.

She blushed again and shook her head. "No, it isn't that. It's just that I can't eat this much." She said as she looked at her plate. The brothers groaned and took her plate from her. They took away the mountains they had placed on her plate in the first place. They all ate together, and silence was a big factor. Aurora looked at the clock on the wall. Her flight was at three and it was now eleven. She ate quickly and fussed about the time. When they had finished all together, Aurora had asked Tristan to take her to her car. He had agreed and disappeared to his room.

Aurora stayed in the living room with Manny and watched TV. She cuddled next to him, and he wrapped his arm around her.

"You're not telling him you're leaving today huh?" He whispered.

She tensed up and felt as if she was going to cry. "How did you know?" she said as she looked up at him. He smiled faintly and pulled her into a tight hug.

"You told my parents you were leaving in two days, but I know you better than that. You're leaving today since you can't take this anymore. I understand. Just promise me something? Be careful out there. It's a tough world babe." He said as he kissed her head lightly.

She curled up closer to him and felt content. It felt nice to have someone to rely on. She was too ungrateful. She didn't deserve people like Manny who wasted their time caring about her. "Thanks, Manny. I promise I will. But you have something to promise me too." She said as she latched onto him.

Manny looked down at her and smiled. "What? Do you want to use me to make an ex-boyfriend jealous? If that's it, I'm so there." He said with a grin.

She punched him in the stomach and rolled her eyes. "No but good try. I need you not to mention it to Tristan. He'll find out but I don't want him to find out before I leave here." she said softly.

She heard Tristan shut the door to his room and she looked up at Manny pleadingly. He looked down at her and smiled. "I promise." He whispered just as Tristan approached.

"Ready Aurora?" he said as he laced his sneakers. She stood up and hugged the young man next to her.

"Bye Man." She whispered as she pulled away from him. Her eyes watered and she felt small tears threaten to spill out.

"Bye Aur. Take care of yourself." He said as he watched her walk away. Tristan and she walked outside and to his car. She looked back at the house and felt a sinking feeling inside. She got into the car and didn't bother to look at the house again.

They drove through town and Aurora felt her heart pound miserably. She knew she would have said goodbye at some point, but it was hopeless. She was holding more pain than she had the first time. She turned to him slowly and took note of his changed appearance. He matured and she hadn't had a close-up look at him. To her, he was still the same man she had loved many years ago. She watched as his eyes flickered around and shot at her briefly. The good feeling about that time was she knew her that love for him was strong. She wanted to leave but at the same time, she didn't want to leave him without telling him about her whereabouts. She wanted him to chase her and show that he still cared about her, so they'd be able to sort out their problems. It was too late for that. Her stubborn mind had already protested against her heart, and she knew it was settled. It was easy to say her heart and mind were disjointed.

She looked out the window of his car and turned her body away from him. Her mind was screwed up and her heart was being unreasonable. She didn't know what she wanted. It always came down to her gut feeling. She knew that even though it wasn't always the best choice, she had no other one. It was too late for her. She was already heartbroken and secluded.

As they neared the bar Aurora felt a dull ache in her head. She didn't want to run away from this place again, but she had to. It was part of her job and also part of her emotions. The car came to a stop and Aurora closed her eyes. This was it. Another goodbye she didn't want to happen. She turned and looked over at Tristan who was smiling at her. The glint in his eyes died out as he saw her blanched expression.

"What's wrong?" He said confused.

She forced a smile and threw her unhappy mood away. "Nothing. I was just thinking if anything happened last night I need to remember." she said with a shrug. He smiled and parked his car next to hers. They stepped out of the car and felt the cool breeze sway around them. She shivered a bit and refrained from crying. She was going to miss the unruly weather. She grabbed her purse out of his car and dug into it to find her keys. She found them and opened her car slowly. She tried to stall her time to be able to stay with him longer. She wanted him to hug her and hold her tight, but it was practically impossible. She placed everything in her car and closed her eyes again. She faced him and his eyes glittered dangerously.

"Why so tense?" He said with a smile.

"I'm not." She replied sharply.

Tristan grinned and shook his head. "If you say so." he said softly.

Aurora felt her heart clench and she bit her lip. "Yeah well, I have to go. Thanks for everything." She said with a smile. She entered her car and rolled the window down. Tristan watched her and smiled kindly.

"See you around Aur." He said happily.

"Goodbye Tristan." She whispered. She eyed his happy expression once more and drove away with a heart full of guilt. When she had got to her house, she had no more tears left. Her eyes had been too swollen, and it felt drier than ever. She dragged herself out of her car and headed inside the house. She walked around the house in search of Renee and was shocked to find her in her room reading a book. Renee had brightened when she saw Aurora but had become worried as she saw her blue eyes cloudier than ever. Aurora had exploded onto the bed, and she couldn't tell if there was a new batch of tears ready to fall. Renee had patted her back lightly and watched her sympathetically. When Aurora had finally stopped crying, she was helped by Renee's smile.

"Sweetie, what's wrong." she said kindly.

Aurora looked up at her and felt a small smile escape her. "I'm leaving in a few hours. I said bye to Tristan, but he didn't know I was leaving. Only his younger brother and you know. I'm going to tell my mom too. Renee, I need you to not tell a soul about it, okay? You can leave when you want but don't tell anyone or hint anything out to them. The next time I'm going to be here is for the wedding and I'm going to leave right after the wedding anyway." She said with a shaky voice.

Renee nodded and held her close to her. "I promise Aur. Now we have got to get you ready. You're going to be late if you don't get ready." Renee said as she stood up. Renee pulled her suitcases out from under her bed and tossed all her belongings into it. Aurora lay on her bed once more and stared at the ceiling. "Renee, when are you planning to go back to FL?" she said wearily.

Renee craned her neck towards Aurora and shrugged. "Maybe tomorrow or the next day; I promise I'll go back." she said with a quirky smile. Aurora rolled her eyes and grabbed the tattered monkey she loved. Its soft fur had thinned over the years and the thread holding its arm was tearing. "Aur, you should go say something to your mom," Renee said as she closed the suitcases.

She smiled and nodded. "I will right now. Get me a new set of clothes, will you? I've been wearing this since yesterday." Aurora said sweetly.

Renee rolled her eyes and nodded. "You are so lucky you have me." She whispered as Aurora walked away.

Aurora walked down the halls and searched for her mom who happened to be in her room. She entered the room, and she saw her sitting on her bed typing on a computer. She looked up at Aurora when she heard the door open and smiled at her. "Hey Aur. What happened to you last night?" Maria said with a mischievous smile. Aurora blushed and neared her mother. She had told her the whole story and her mother had a soft expression on her face. When she had finished, she wasn't able to tell if her mom was shocked or not. "So… you and Tristan? Truthfully, I always like that boy. Now you're leaving again huh? Just make sure you visit me once in a while. I get lonely around here." Maria said with a sincere smile. Aurora kissed her mom's cheek and walked away slowly. "Hey Aur?" she said hesitantly.

Aurora stopped in her tracks and looked back. "Yeah?" she asked.

Her mom smiled and replied with a shrug, "Don't lose someone you can't stop thinking about. Maybe he's supposed to be around." Aurora nodded and walked away with more on her mind than before.

When she had taken a shower and changed her clothes, she felt renewed. She knew her time home was ending. Renee had left her room and had been waiting in the living room. Aurora looked around the room and she set her eyes onto the wall of pictures. She wanted to take all the pictures with her, but she had a big sense of hesitation. She smiled once again as she viewed them and walked to the door. She leaned against the door frame and looked back at her room. Her mind flew back to a moment in time when she had sat in her bed and talked to her girlfriends about their latest crushes. When she told them about Tristan, they were shocked. They all confessed to their crushes, and she had to admit most of the time she had been shocked. It was all in the past now. Nothing was able to be changed. She smiled at the room and shut the door, ready to come back to her reality.

She walked down the hallways and toward her mother's room. She had given her mom a brief goodbye which left her mother in tears. Her promise to be back had made her mom smile. Within minutes, Renee and she were driving off towards the airport. Aurora had told her about the day before. She had tried to dig up the missing pieces of the puzzle, but everything seemed to be intact. They drove through the town and Aurora viewed the buildings and the people walking by. It was goodbye for now, but she knew it wasn't the last of her memorable city. When they had reached the airport, Renee had tried as quickly as she could to get rid of her.

"Go Aur. You're going to be late. I'll see you in two days anyway. Don't do anything stupid okay?" Renee said as she quickly drove off before the airport police officers got to her. Aurora stood at the curb and watched as Renee disappear from her sight.

She entered the airport and took in the busy lifestyle she had been too accustomed to. She walked to her designated wing and with each breath her heartbeat mellowed. She couldn't shake the last image of Tristan she had. The way he looked so ruffled and confused when she drove away a little bit too quickly. She felt as if she had left her heart with him, and he hadn't accepted it. He had it without knowing. Then, there was her father. He hadn't even tried to talk to her. She mentally shook herself and sighed in relief. Now it was time for her to leave. Reality was calling and it was her obligation to follow it.

Chapter 21

Within another hour, Aurora was on an airplane and flying high in the blue sky. She looked out from her seat next to the window. She saw land and water while peeping through the open window. She sat and looked over at the kind old lady who was sitting next to her. Aurora pulled a magazine out of her bag and read the latest entertainment news. She came to a page that had Mike smiling flirtatiously. His eyes flickered with amusement as he held a phone to his ear. Aurora groaned and threw the magazine onto the empty seat beside her. An elderly woman looked up at her and smiled at her sympathetically. "Man problems?" the woman said with a knowing look. She nodded and smiled faintly. The woman laughed quietly and stuck her hand out. "Maggie Jensen."

Aurora took her hand and smiled. "Aurora Mathews." she said sweetly. The old woman's eyes broadened and she smiled widely. "Aurora. Weren't you the one who dated that rich man who works in Miami? Oh, what is his name? Mike! Mike Kline?" Maggie said as she threw her hands up in a cheer.

Aurora nodded and smiled sourly. "Yeah, that's one but it's really about another guy, not him," Aurora said with a deep sigh.

Maggie pulled her purse from under her seat and set it on her lap. She grabbed a bar of chocolate out and handed it to her. Aurora gave her a questioning look and took the chocolate.

"Chocolate always helps." She said with a big smile. Aurora nodded. Maggie smiled happily and pulled out a book and pen from her bag. She started writing quickly and took sneaky looks at Aurora.

"May I ask what you're doing?" she asked with a kind tone. Maggie looked up at her blankly. "Writing, I thought it was very obvious," Maggie said as she rolled her hazel eyes.

Aurora smiled and shook her head. "No, I was wondering what you are writing," Aurora said as she looked closer.

Maggie gave her the book and Aurora read the first pages. It was a love story. It had depth to it and Aurora felt a stirring feeling inside her. "It isn't a fake story. It's my love life in a nutshell. I never shared it with anyone besides you. I think it's because you interest me." Maggie smiled.

Aurora looked up at her with a questioning look. "I'm nothing near interesting," Aurora said with a bashful tone.

Maggie laughed sweetly and shook her head. "Of course, you don't think you are. Leave it to other people to tell you." Maggie said.

Aurora read the book …

"They say you remember everything or should I say your first everything. As for myself, there is no way I can forget that kiss our first kiss…ever. I had to laugh at myself just now, I felt like a giddy schoolgirl remembering it. Yes, I know it's childish to be giddy like that after so many years, but you'll understand once you know what happened to make me feel that way or in truth what makes me feel that way till this day every time he touches me. The Super Bowl is a night of excitement especially when it's your team in the game and they win. It could have been the euphoric atmosphere or any number of things happening at the moment. To this day, knowing all I know I still can't explain the feeling correctly.

It was something like out of a movie. The minute our eyes locked the rest of the world disappeared. The magnetic pull between us was so intense when our lips connected the kiss itself was electrified. Jolts were running through my body and amid all those sensations I felt complete... totally and completely... complete. If it wasn't for our friend's mother commenting about breaking lights. When our lips touched the electricity was so intense it broke the light above our heads. Crazy right? I would have never believed it. It was too weird to be coincidental. We didn't even notice it happened until it was pointed out. I know it might seem like a crazy story to believe hell it was crazy being a part of it. Nonetheless, at that moment I knew I loved him, and I would never love another. I had found my soul mate better, yet I realized I had found my twin flame." It felt as if Maggie had been through exactly what she had.

Love seemed to pour out of the pages as she explained about a man she had fallen in love with. Aurora felt as if it was a book waiting to be published; only it was like a diary. It was the deep inner thoughts that a woman didn't bother to share aloud. She handed it back to Maggie and the woman took it with a smile.

"Now that I shared my story, care to share yours?"

Chapter 22

When the flight was over, Aurora felt better. She knew if she told someone who knew how her life worked, they would have been exasperated. Telling Maggie was the smartest thing she had done. The woman listened and distributed things that were exactly what Aurora wanted to hear. Meeting someone like her was a lucky thing. She walked around the airport and watched as people rushed around her. She felt different from when she had left. She had that feeling like she didn't belong, but this was her real life. The busy feeling and the rush were what she had been used to. She knew she had been far away from the feeling for too long. She walked along and sat on a bench waiting for a cab. She watched as a man with plain jeans and a flannel shirt sat next to her. He had sunglasses on, and he crossed his arms over his chest. He seemed familiar, but Aurora couldn't put her finger on it.

"You shouldn't stare Aur. If it weren't me, the person would have thought you're a creep." The man said as he lowered his sunglasses. Piercing eyes peeped out from the shades and Aurora groaned.

"Maybe I wouldn't care what they thought Mike," Aurora said with a cold stare.

Mike pulled off his shades and shook his head. "Nice to see you too sweetheart no need to be so hostile. I have known you for a year and then we went out for months. We even got engaged and yet you act like I'm a total stranger. What went wrong between us?" he said lightly.

Aurora felt her head pulse and shook her head lightly. "Why are you here? How did you know I'd be here today?" She said as all warning bells turned on in her mind.

"Why don't I give you a ride home? I'll tell you everything you want to know, and I expect some answers too." Mike said as he stood up. He placed his shades on her face again and held out his hand in front of her. She took it hesitantly and watched as the crowds of people around them watched. He carried her suitcase in one hand and held her hand in the other. His grip around her was warm and reassuring her that he was there for her. She knew her eventual answer when it came to them. They walked along the sidewalk and came to his car. He placed her bags in the back and opened her door for her. She got in and before he closed the door she stopped him.

"Decided to lie low and not bring that limo of yours?" Aurora said teasingly.

He rolled his eyes and smiled. "Yeah, is that alright princess?" he said as he leaned against the door.

Aurora smiled and looked up at him hesitantly. "More than alright thanks." She said as she bit her lip. Mike closed the door and walked around to his seat. She did know how to wind him up. The only problem was whether it was good or bad.

Tristan drove up into his parents' driveway and smiled to himself. Things between him and Aurora were lightening up. She had even kissed him even if she hadn't taken note of it. He wished she weren't so drunk that she wasn't able to feel it. It was the closest thing to heaven. He walked to the door with a smile plastered on his face and it felt as if everything was working for them. He walked into the house and tried to find his brother. He heard his brother in the kitchen with his mom. Tristan walked up to them slowly and heard them whisper.

"She's gone, mom. He doesn't even know it yet but by now she's probably on a plane going back home." He heard Manny whisper. His heart pounded and a dull pain shot in his head. They couldn't be talking about Aurora. She would have told me. Wouldn't she? He went into panic mode and clenched his scarf. She would have told me, right? He thought with more heartache.

"Who's gone?" Tristan said loudly as he walked into the kitchen. His mom and brother looked up at him with wide eyes and smiled forcefully.

"How much did you hear?" Manny said with a frown.

Tristan leaned against the doorway and frowned equally. "Enough to wonder who is leaving." He said monotonously.

"It's um a girl in my class. Yeah, I had a crush on her." Manny said as his eyes flickered to their mom worriedly. Tristan looked at his brother wearily and shook his head.

"Man, you always sucked at lying. So, I'm going to ask Mom." He said as he turned to his mom. His mom stared at him and shook her head sadly.

"I can't tell you." His mom said as she stood up and walked toward her bedroom. Manny looked up at him wearily and gazed at him sharply. "I'm sorry bro." He said as he stood up.

Tristan groaned and felt that same heartache he had before. "She left, didn't she?" He said with a sad smile. Manny nodded and placed his hand on his brother's shoulder. He walked away and Tristan stood in the empty kitchen. He thought everything was working out for them. It wasn't. Even though she was gone, she took his heart with her.

"So where have you been this whole time?" Mike asked as they stopped in traffic.

"I was in my hometown." She said with a melancholy tone. Mike looked over at her and frowned.

"Was it bad?" he asked as he ran his hand through his hair.

"It was one of the best times of my life. I met up with my old friends and I talked with my mom." she said with a deep sigh. She didn't want to mention Tristan even though he was a highlight of her trip.

"Your mom? How did that go?" he said kindly. She smiled.

"Better than you would have thought." She said with a chuckle. They talked with each other till the traffic eased up. "Now you have to answer my questions. How did you know I was coming back today?" she asked as they came around to her house. He parked the car and replied,

"I called the restaurant. Your boss told me you were on vacation, and you were coming back today. I'm such a resourceful person, am I not?" he said with a grin.

Aurora rolled her eyes, and they walked into the house. Mike carried all her belongings into her living room and they both sat in the kitchen. She thought back to what Renee had told her. Did she just want to drop him out of her life? She didn't know but she knew whatever had happened between them before was in the past. Even if there was a spark of love in there, she didn't feel it anymore.

"Let's talk," Aurora said as she leaned back in her chair Mike gulped and shook his head.

"It feels like you're breaking up with me again don't sugarcoat it get to the point Aur." He said with a grim smile.

"I just wanted to know what you wanted to talk about." she said sharply.

Mike reached for her hand and took it between his hands. "Tell me why you don't want to be with me." He said sadly.

"When did I say I didn't want to be with you? Not to give you any ideas but I haven't said it directly yet." She said with a frown.

Mike chuckled and smiled widely. "I just know you more than I wanted to. It's written all over your face." He said with a smile.

Aurora shrugged unconsciously and smiled. "Well, it doesn't mean I don't want to be your friend." she said as she withdrew her hand slowly.

Her phone rang and she pulled it out of her purse. She placed it on the table and looked at the screen. It was Tristan. He already knew she was gone, and it had been only six hours since she left. She groaned and threw her phone back into her purse.

"Your office?" Mike said with a small smile.

Aurora shot him a glare and replied, "It's worse than that."

He grinned and pulled her bag to him. "Let's see about that." He said as he pulled her bag out from her bag. She tried to tackle him for it, but he was too quick for his good. He read the screen and gave her a quizzical look.

"And who, may I ask, is Tristan Alvarez?" he said with a grin.

Aurora blushed from the roots of her hair to the tip of her toes. "Someone." She mumbled. He held the phone close to her and the ringing stopped. It beeped and a message had been recorded. Mike opened her phone and called her voicemail. She had no energy to stop him and watched as he dialed in her password. "How the hell do you know my password?" she grumbled.

He grinned and shook his head. "That's what happens when you get engaged to someone. My life is like yours. Well, was." He said as he placed the phone on speaker. She finally heard Manny's deep voice and barely caught what he said.

"Hi Aur. Okay, I bet you were expecting Tristan, but he's too torn up to say anything. I know I promised I wouldn't tell him, but I had to. He sort of overheard my mom and I talking about you and well he squeezed it out of me. I'm sorry. If you think you're the only one torn up about all those years ago then you should have seen him. Even now you shouldn't have left. It's not too late to start over Aurora. Remember that." She heard over the phone. The message ended and she froze up. So, he was upset over her leaving for the second time. How could she miss that? Mike hung up the phone and looked up at her expectantly.

"Come on Aur. You can tell me. Sounds like you found someone new?" he said with a grin.

Aurora glared at him and played with her necklace. "He's not new. I've known him all my life. He was my first love." she said as a small smile played across her lips. Mike looked at her surprised and leaned in for more detail.

"Explain more, would you?" he said lightly. Aurora closed her eyes and thought of something to say.

"We started dating in high school things happened and he called quits. I loved him and he broke my heart a typical love life. That's when I decided to leave my hometown and move here. I saw him a lot when I was home for the past two weeks and I really can't get him off my mind." she said stubbornly.

Mike leaned back and smiled broadly. "Ah, so he was the only one who got inside your heart? I get it. So why did you run away without telling him? Didn't you think about how he would have felt?" Mike said drastically. He was a sucker for romance.

Aurora rolled her eyes and replied, "How was I supposed to know how he felt? I left mostly because of him, and I got nothing. I waited years for him to say something to me and nothing. I want him to chase after me and realize that I wanted him to make a move for a long time. But no, men are so insensitive to the way women feel." He looked at her in disgust and snorted.

"Please. Women do the same. Just give him a chance, Aurora. Maybe he's just thinking things through." he said with a frown.

"Mike, if he is thinking things through, it's been years. He could have just told me how he felt while I was there but instead, he sent me weird signs. I can't wait for an answer anymore." she said dully.

He shook his head and smiled. "Wait just a little longer. It might be the best thing that happens to you."

Jezza Deep

Chapter 23

Tristan left within the next week to go back home. Aurora burned her way into his mind whenever he didn't have a thought in his mind. Now he had to break it off with Penny. He had just arrived home. His office had given him extra time off, so he had a week left of his break. As he walked out of the airport, the busy city embraced him with snow. He felt the small snowflakes drift slowly onto his face. He looked up at the sky and watched the snowflakes fall to the ground as if they were in a slow dance. His first errand was Penny. He walked along the cold snow-filled ground toward the lines of cabs. He hailed a cab and entered the car full of warmth. A balding man in his fifties looked over his shoulder at him and nodded. "Where to?" he said in a gruff voice.

Tristan closed his eyes and recited his address. They drove in silence beside the soft rock music in the background. When they reached his house, he paid the driver. He walked up the steps outside his apartment and smiled. Home sweet home, he thought with a smile. He walked into his house and turned on the lights only to see a waiting, Penny. When he looked up at her, the first thing he noticed was her immaculately curled hair and tight clothing. He looked straight at her face full of makeup and cringed. She stood in front of him with her hands on her hips and frowned.

"Where have you been Tristan? I have been trying to find you for weeks." She whined. Tristan wanted to punch the wall but reigned in his emotions.

"None of your business Penny, we're not entirely an item so why bother asking for my whereabouts?" he said coldly.

She walked toward him, and her heels clacked onto the wood floor annoyingly. It took a lot for Tristan to not run away from her entirely. She giggled and sat on a chair close to the front door. "Oh Tristan, you are so funny! I knew where you were anyway so no need to explain. And please!! You and I are so perfect for each other." She said in a pouty voice.

He clenched his fists tightly and looked up at her square in the eye. "If you're done now, please leave and stay out of my life forever because I would rather jump off a bridge than be with you." he said as he opened the door wide.

She marched up to the edge of the threshold and turned back at him with a spiteful gaze. "You'll regret losing me, Tristan Alvarez." She said in an icy tone. She stepped onto the first step out of his house and turned her whole body toward the door. Tristan shut the door halfway and stuck his head out of the open part. He grinned knowingly and shook his head.

"I already found someone I'm willing to spend the rest of my life with." He said with a smug look. He shut the door on her dumbstruck face and smiled to himself, knowing he had one last hurdle to jump.

Weeks turned into a month and Aurora was expected back home for Tina and Jack's wedding. Within the time she was back at her home, Aurora realized she did need Mike around. He was a good friend to her and even offered to go with her. Renee was going as well and was more than happy to visit Max. The two had bonded on Renee's last day there and hit off almost too well. They kept their relationship strong as they talked over the phone nonstop every day. Aurora also talked to him, and he mentioned how Tristan had been before he left also to go back to Philly. Max had explained how Tristan put up a tough front but had hidden those problems deep inside him. Aurora felt drastically responsible for the pain that was caused him. She knew seeing him would be hard, but she had to get through it. It was the same feeling she had the first time around and yet incredibly different. This time she knew it was her fault even if she still felt he was responsible.

She left her heart with him at the same time blamed him for taking it, even if he had no idea. Now, as she was packing her bags, a feeling of guilt washed over her.

"You ready yet? We have to start moving if you want an extra day to rest." Mike said as he entered her room.

Aurora nodded slowly and walked around her room in search of clothing. Within those few weeks, she had become withdrawn. Renee had said it was a reminder of what had happened when she had first moved there. She felt arms wrapped around her body and smiled faintly.

"Don't act like this Aur. You are going to see this Tristan and you guys will work out your problems and all will end well. Got it??" he said as he hugged her tightly.

Aurora smiled and slumped against his chest. "If he even shows up." she said gloomily.

"He will be. You were the one who told me he wouldn't miss this wedding even if his life depended on it." Mike said annoyed. For the last few weeks, Mike was practically her secretary. He made sure she was intact and lively when she went to work and that her emotions didn't get the better of her. Renee had also done the same and had to smack sense into her more than once. It was a nice feeling, but she still had that feeling of regret on the layer of her thoughts.

"I know. I just wish that this wedding meant less to me so I wouldn't have to go. Instead, I get chosen to be a bridesmaid and have to be near him." she said in disgust.

Mike reached down and kissed her head as a friendly sign of affection. "Don't worry about it. You have your other friends, Renee and me, there to back you up. Are you sure I won't stir up rumors? I mean we were about to get married. Tristan might sense something's still here." He said as he pointed from her back to him.

Aurora giggled and shook her head. "If that's your way of saying you're scared, don't be. You might stir up rumors, but we will instantly kill them out by saying you have a girlfriend here. You can name her what you want. Just be sure to tell me since I might mess up and say another name." She responded.

Mike smiled and let go of her. "Alright now hurry up so we can head out." He walked out of her room and Aurora stared out the window with a smile. The blue sky brightened her mood as she watched the birds flying above. She was ready for all that was coming when it came to Tristan.

Chapter 24

The drive to NJ was relaxing yet made Aurora more confused. Mike and Renee were raving about the vast fields and the millions of cows they had seen which might have been their next meal if the cows didn't count their blessings. Aurora's mind had kept drifting to Tristan, but they had immediately pulled her away from her thoughts as soon as they saw a familiar look on her face. He was all she could think about. She was furious at herself and yet still held her anger toward him for those years he didn't try to chase after her. What was she going to do? Maybe her mom was right. Maybe he was supposed to be in her head. Maybe this time around she was the one who screwed up, not him. She groaned inwardly and realized they were within nine miles of the city. Her pulse raced and her mind pounded loudly.

This was it. She thought it would be easy, but her body cowered as her mind became strong. She knew she was going to crash and burn during the whole phase. She was a disaster waiting to happen. She felt an arm come around her shoulders and pull her toward their body. She looked up at Mike who smiled at her faintly. She did know how much he had been a victim in her cold ways and gave him admiration for sticking up to her and cooling her down. She leaned against him and sighed.

"I'm sorry if it didn't work out between us because of me." He said genuinely.

Aurora shook her head and smiled faintly. "It wasn't entirely you. You can blame me for having such a big ego. Plus, I didn't realize how much I was holding onto Tristan in my heart. It was unfair to you Mike." She whispered gently. Mike nodded and looked around as they entered the dreary city.

Renee had opened all the windows and let them view the city limits. Aurora pointed out places where she had most of her memories and Mike listened intently. Renee drove up to Maria's house and they sat in the car and viewed the house with small smiles.

"This is where it all started?" Mike asked as he stepped out of the car.

Aurora stepped out as well and nodded. "Yeah, it is. Now let's go meet my mother, shall we?" she said as she reached for Mike's arm. They walked all together towards the door and Aurora rang the bell. She heard a clatter behind the door, and it opened showing her mother.

"Aurora!! I've missed you!!" her mother said as she charged at her. She hugged her tightly and Aurora forgot to breathe. When her mom let go, she hugged Renee as she did to Aurora. They entered the house, and her mother gave Mike a look over. "You must be Mike." She said in half disgust and half amusement.

Mike cringed and smiled at her widely. "Yeah, I am." He said with a grin. Maria grinned and walked away quickly. Mike sat on the sofa and looked around the room. "Aurora this place is freaking gigantic. My house isn't even this big and I'm scared of your mom. She looks like she hates me." He said as he looked at the next room.

Aurora grinned and pulled him off the couch. "You haven't seen anything yet and Mom doesn't hate you, she's just like that," she said as she pulled him toward her room. They all climbed up the stairs and stood in front of her room. Mike looked at the pictures on the door and smiled. She opened the door, and they entered her room.

"I knew you would have a girly room." He said as he viewed the room. Renee snorted and walked away down to the kitchen. He walked to the pictures and viewed each one. He came to a picture of Aurora with a guy. She was smiling brightly as the guy kissed the corner of her mouth. He hadn't seen that side of her as much as he intended to. He thought jealousy would hit him, but he only felt happiness in looking at that picture. He knew that it was Tristan in the picture with her. "Is that him?" he said as he pointed to the picture. He heard something fall onto the bed and turned to see Aurora lying on top of it tiredly.

"Yep, that is the famous Tristan Alvarez." she said as she groaned into a pillow. Mike turned back to the picture and smiled. It was nice seeing that Aurora had a vulnerable side to her stoic façade. He walked away from the wall and sat on the edge of the bed. She sat up to hug her knees and looked over at him.

"Are you ready for all of this? Life gets complicated when you're around me." She whispered.

Mike chuckled lightly and shook his head. "I think this is fun." He said with a smile. Aurora smiled wearily and watched as he stood up and stretched. He had no idea what his family and friends could be. He patted her leg softly and walked down the halls slowly. She curled up and hugged her knees tightly.

"This is too stupid. I hate my life." She said loudly.

"Well, I have to admit you always had bumps in the road. What could be new?" A deep voice said. She looked up and saw Jack smiling down at her.

"Jack! You're here!" she said as she tackled him against the doorway. He laughed melodiously and hugged her firmly.

"Hey, beautiful." he said in his deep voice. Aurora pulled away from him and laughed. His eyes were as bright as the sky on a clear sunny day.

"Well, hello, handsome. How's the fiancée?" she said with a grin.

He cringed and paced around the room. "Well, she's Bridezilla and she's tired so it adds fuel to her fire. She gets mad so easily. I can't wait to get this wedding over with." He sighed as he walked around briskly.

Aurora nodded and smiled in agreement. "Tomorrow's the big day. My little boys are all grown up." she said with a deep sigh.

Jack pulled out a chair and slouched himself onto it. "Yeah, to tell the truth, I'm overwhelmed. I'm marrying my dream girl, I have my dream job, and my best friends are all here for my wedding. What more could I want?" he said dreamily.

"Children?" she asked with a smile. He looked up at her with a pale face and shook his head.

"Not yet. I feel ancient thinking about it." he said with a forced smile. Aurora nodded and took a seat on her bed.

A moment of silence filled the room, and she busied herself with a teddy bear. "Why did you have to leave so suddenly? You promised you would tell me if you left again." Jack asked in a whisper.

Aurora shrugged and played with the monkey's torn ear. "I had a problem at work to deal with and maybe Tristan was a big part of it. I didn't tell you because it was a… I decided to leave then boarded a plane immediately." She said in a whisper.

Jack groaned and stood up from the chair. "I wonder when the both of you will finally grow up and see the whole picture! Both of you are running away from what you both want! It's so foolish." He said in a stern voice.

Aurora looked up from the stuffed animal and felt her heart ablaze. "Maybe it's because he never showed any sign that he was chasing after me huh? I have all those stupid regrets in my mind, but what about him? Is he sorry for any of it? With the way he just broke my heart without warning or reason and sent me into a depressed state, I doubt it. So yeah, I still can be madly in love with him, but he needs to be following the same path. If he wants me then he come and get me. He's already had millions of chances to. You don't understand any of it." she said angrily.

It always came to this. Everyone had asked why they just couldn't be together. It was more complicated than they knew. Her life wasn't some stupid romance novel that came to a happy conclusion. There were hard times and they weren't leaving unless Tristan noticed how stupid his actions had been. It wasn't just because he broke up with her years ago. He left her alone when she needed someone to be her anchor. She knew it was a biased feeling inside of her and yet she didn't care.

"Then help me understand!!" he yelled. Aurora eyed him scornfully. "I'm not trying to defend him but he's only human Aur." He said in a whisper.

Aurora buried her head in the monkey and smirked. "Yeah, I know. This visit will help to see if our relationship will move forward or finally end." She said with a sigh. Jack eyed her wearily and nodded.

Chapter 25

"Look, I'm sorry sweetie but you need to breathe. You aren't even married to the guy yet and you're bawling buckets. He probably only went out with Max and Ant. Tonight's the bachelor party and they're probably getting ready." Tristan said to Tina.

She looked up at him with her bloodshot eyes and gulped visibly. "Ant and Max said they wouldn't need him until tonight! I'm a mess, Tris!" She cried. She hunched forward onto her chair and Tristan patted her back lightly. She cried louder and he felt his ears prickle from her shrill sobs.

"He's been going through the same things so don't worry. You both went through the same fatigue so don't cry. He's willing to stick around, no matter what." Tristan replied as her sobs wore down.

She looked up at him helplessly and he frowned. He wiped away a stray tear on her cheek and a smile opened slowly onto her face. "I leave for less than an hour and I see my best friend making moves on my love. Bad move man." Tristan heard from behind him. He grinned and shook his head quickly.

"You can have her. I was just making sure to fill in a void while it was available." He said with a grin. Jack walked over to them and Tristan stood up, waving the now open seat to him. Jack sat down and eyed his weeping fiancé.

"What's wrong baby?" he asked as he reached for her hand. She pulled away from him and crossed her arms. She turned and looked at Tristan feebly. He gave her a knowing look and Tina looked back at Jack. "I'm just really tired I guess." She whispered. Jack raised his eyebrow in judgment. Tina was plain stubborn when she wanted to be. He could tell she was upset over him being gone for a long time without telling her.

He didn't want to spoil the surprise that Aurora was there so luckily, he brought a tiny gift in compensation and as an alibi. "I'll try to believe that. Now turn around and close your eyes." He said with a grin. Tina's eyes widened and she turned around slowly. "Now stay here while I get something from downstairs. Don't open your eyes." He said as he fled from the room. Tina sighed and a small smile blossomed across her face.

"You are such a woman," Tristan said as he watched her smile.

Tina giggled and shook her head. "If you want to woo a woman, Tris, you got to know how to do things like Jack. Or even better, just tell the truth and be yourself." She replied with her smile still plastered on her face. Tristan grinned and shook his head at the woman in love. Jack came back and kneeled in front of her.

"Open your eyes now." He said as he pulled something from his pocket. She opened her eyes and looked at the ring in a velvet case. She gasped loudly and looked as if she was going to cry again. "I didn't give you a proper ring when I proposed to you, so I hope it isn't too late to give you this." He said as he slid the ring onto her finger. She jumped from her seat and hugged him tightly. He fell back and they rolled around on the floor happily.

Tristan laughed and walked down the hallway. "I'm leaving now!! Don't get too tired before tonight, Jack!" he shouted from down the stairs. He walked out of the house and toward his car. He looked out at the blue skies and leaned against his car. For the first time in a while, Aurora had popped into his mind. He didn't know where they left off. It was a plain goodbye and he had no clue she was leaving. If only he knew then. He would have stopped her and told her how he felt. He felt like an idiot for not chasing after her. He knew that was what she wanted and yet he couldn't give her that one thing. He entered his car and drove away planning his actions out.

Aurora had decided to take Mike on a walk around the city. She placed sunglasses on him but knew people would notice him. She dragged him throughout the city, and he insisted on holding her hand so he wouldn't get lost. Before there would be sparks everywhere when he held it now the friendly gesture just to keep her hands warm. She pulled him in from store to store and watched as the people around them eyed them curiously. She didn't care. It was too much fun she didn't want to care that much. They looked at the shop's merchandise and laughed when something looked too hideous. They tried on different hats and shades and when they walked along the sidewalks of the street they would laugh loudly, and they never cared who stopped to stare. It was their day to do whatever they wanted. They sat down near the park where she held most of her memories.

She looked as two teens swung on the swings happily and then jumped off to hug each other tightly. "Isn't that the park in the picture?" Mike said as he took off his shades. Aurora nodded and slumped back against her seat. "Where did Renee go? I haven't seen her since we got here." he asked with a smile.

Aurora grinned and replied, "Probably went to see Max." He nodded and viewed his surroundings carefully.

"This place is really beautiful." He said as he looked around. She stood up and smiled at him.

"It gets better. C'mon," she said as she held out her hand to him. He took her hand stubbornly and listened to her babbling as she dragged him around. Aurora caught sight of a black Maserati parked on the sidewalk. The car was parked in front of a flower boutique. She knew he wouldn't have been in there. "Mike, listen to me right now. That car belongs to Tristan. He could be anywhere so when I tell you he's around, do something to help me out. You're a movie producer. I think you can think of something clever to get him." she said with a devious grin.

Mike rolled his eyes and smiled the same smile. "How do you know that it's him for sure?" he asked.

"Because I do, he is in love with that car. Trust me it's his" she said with a grin. Mike shrugged and nodded. He held his hand out toward her, and she grabbed it. He pulled her along the street, and they headed straight toward the boutique.

"I didn't agree to this." She panicked. She pulled her hand away from him and walked away. She didn't look up when she walked away and ran straight into a tall person. She almost fell back but they caught her by the waist.

"Careful there, ma'am." She heard a deep voice say. Shit, she thought silently. She knew that voice anywhere and anytime. It haunted her for the last month, and she wanted to wait one more day before actually facing him. She tilted her head downward and avoided his strong gaze.

"I'm sorry. My girlfriend here is a klutz. Come dear." She heard Mike say behind her. She didn't look up at him and he loosened his grip on her waist. She turned away quickly, and Mike reached for her hand. They walked away, their backs facing him.

"I wonder if he realized that it was you." he said as he tightened his grip on her hand.

Aurora felt her heartbeat unconsciously and her face burned. She turned back briefly, and eyed Tristan had the same ruffled look as he had before she left. "Oh, he knows it was me alright."

Chapter 26

No way, Tristan thought with a grudging frown. That was her. That was the woman who had him wrapped around her finger. She had been the star of most of his dreams and nightmares. And she was with that playboy. What the hell was happening here? Did she get back together with him? For one month, he had been fussing and planning how to win her back to only be bumped back to square one. What was he going to do? He watched as they walked away quickly down the sidewalk, and he eyed their intertwined hands. She was so frail looking, and he felt as if she had lost weight. When he had caught her, her body was shaking. She didn't even look up at him. As they disappeared from his sight, he jumped into his car and took out his phone. He called Renee immediately and waited for her to answer. "Hello?" he heard over the phone. "Tell me she isn't really with him." Tristan pleaded into the phone.

"Tristan? What are you talking about?" He groaned and slapped his forehead.

"Aurora and that…that guy!!" Tristan shouted into the phone.

His head was pounding and didn't care if he sounded desperate. He was done with all of it. It needed to be figured out.

"No, they aren't. Why? What's wrong Tristan?" he barely heard over the phone.

"She ran into me in town, and I caught her. She acted like she didn't know me and that Mike guy came up and was like 'Oh my girlfriends a klutz I'm sorry.' It pissed me off and now that I know it isn't true I want to punch a wall." he said gravely.

Renee gasped and he heard a voice pipe in. "Sounds like you finally realized you need her in your life Tris," Max said. Tristan grinned and finally took note of what was happening. "Are you two together now? How could you not tell me?" Tristan said with a sigh.

Renee giggled and Tristan heard an audible kiss through the phone. "It was a surprise." He heard Max say in a muffled voice. "Grrreat another mushy couple." He said with disdain.

"Don't worry Tris. After tomorrow we will be the ones complaining about mushy couples. Plus, we haven't seen each other in a month. Give us a break." Renee said happily over the phone.

"You haven't seen me in a month either. Is that the same way you're going to treat me when you see me?" Tristan chuckled.

"Nice try man, but no. She's mine." Max said in a possessive tone. Tristan laughed and hung up. He dropped the phone onto the chair beside him and he drove away with a mind full of thoughts.

Aurora and Mike got back from their walk and felt more tired. Aurora ran up to her room, she entered the house and felt a sense of awareness creep up in her mind. She wanted to stop running. She didn't want this to keep going. It was too tiring, and she just wanted that happy ending. No more tears needed to be shed. She needed to drop her stubborn ways. Even if it was a challenge, she was more determined.

"AURORA MATHEWS!!" she heard from downstairs. She turned back and ran down the stairs to see a blazingly angry woman. "Care to explain your little date in town?" Renee seethed.

Aurora cringed and watched as her friend angrily crossed her arms. The air between them had become hostile and Aurora felt as if she was shrinking in front of the smaller woman.

"I just wanted to show Mike around," Aurora whispered as she looked down at the floor.

Renee huffed impatiently and tapped the top of her heel on the floor. "Yeah, I know that part, but why did you have to hurt Tristan!? The poor guy is in love with you and you-you act like a selfish bitch and walk right over him. I know he hurt you in the past, but you're hurting him more than he deserves." Renee fumed.

Aurora shivered and felt like she was getting stabbed multiple times in the heart. Everything Renee said was true. It had finally hit her. "I know. I'll fix it. That was one of the purposes of coming here." Aurora whispered.

"Good. About time you stopped running away." Renee said as she walked out of the room.

Aurora groaned and fell onto the couch. "She's right you know." came a voice behind her. She sat up and looked at her tired mom.

"Yeah, I know. I wish it were easier though." Aurora said as she plopped back onto the couch again.

"What are you going to do now?" Maria asked with genuine concern.

"I don't know. I guess I'm going to wing it. I work better under pressure." She replied as she turned on the TV. She slouched back onto her seat and felt her body loosen. Her mom walked off with a dramatic sigh and Aurora rolled her eyes, wishing everything were in place.

As the sun rose, the world was still. No sound plagued the house and Aurora rolled onto her back and blinked up at the ceiling. It was still that bleak color, and she remembered when she was staring at it with dread more than a month ago. Not much has changed. Her heart was still rebellious and on fire most of the time. Maybe that was the part of her that couldn't be quenched. Was it stubbornness? She was scared when her dreams sent the wrong messages and felt optimistic when they showed happiness and the things she wanted. Dreams were so powerful to her that she didn't know if any of it would be true. She tried to believe that it was all easier than it seemed, but she psyched herself more when she did. She closed her eyes and thought back to a passage in Maggie Jensen's story...

"I was young. So, I can't say I can make a big deal about being intrigued by many men, but I was constantly surrounded by guys, so you get to read many facets of different male personalities pretty well. His was different from the loud craziness I knew. Strange he kind of didn't fit in personality-wise. He was quiet...shy. The kind you had to poke and prod to get to relax and laugh but when he smiled it lit up a room, staring at it made my entire world feel at peace... strange right? Here I am the hater of men always surrounded by guys who are the definition of crazy and my heart jumps for the shy quiet one. Mind you I am far from shy and quiet, and I am the total opposite of every bit of the fire as the sign I was born under. So, all I kept doing was questioning my sanity.

Every day I would stare at him to figure myself out and eventually, I guess I became obvious. My friend Roe pointed it out to me one beautiful day. "You're in love." was all she said. I turned to her with the most dumbfounded weird expression on my face and replied, "You're CRAZY!" Yes damn, that bitch ended up being right in the end. I swear she started this curse, but it wouldn't be until weeks later that I would find out just how right she was. Better yet it wouldn't be until weeks later I would find out just how fate works in mysterious and devious ways."

Was love really that easy or was I truly that hardened? Now as the sun was barely peeping through the horizon, she felt more worried than before. While at this moment Tina was probably curled up next to her soon-to-be husband and dreaming of her most awaited day, Aurora wasn't so excited. She knew it was a big day because it was her best friend's wedding, but she just couldn't understand her feelings. She was being so selfish and yet nothing was able to change her personal views. She jumped out of the bed and walked to the curtains. She pulled them open and watched as the sun climbed its way into the sky. A new day was beginning. Let's hope it ends like it began.

As soon as ten o'clock struck, Aurora was out the door and heading to Tina's house. She sped her way through the small town and knew she was over the speed limit. She didn't care. The cops knew her, and they were all suckers for tears. All it took was one emotional woman to go overboard on her feelings and break down. She drove her way to Jack and Tina's house and flew up inside the house. Inside was a mess. She heard some yelling and clattering all over the house. She saw dresses lying on the couch and makeup everywhere.

"Thank God you're here!! I thought you'd never show up. I was worried sick!" she heard Tina say as she walked into the same room as Aurora.

She smiled and shrugged her shoulders. "It sounds like a certain bride missed me?" she said with a grin. Tina nodded and hugged her tightly.

"It wouldn't have been the same without you. You complete the whole thing!" Tina said as she pulled Aurora into her room.

She saw Jen, Alexa, and Roxy sitting on the bed and fussing about something. She was surprised to see Renee also. They all hugged, and they got ready. Tina handed Aurora an ivory and black dress full of hand-stitched designs. Aurora thought it was beautiful. She watched as her friends slipped into their matching dresses and looked as dazzling as they intended to be. Aurora felt as if she would have been the sore thumb in the crowd but decided not to care. She slipped into the dress and looked at her figure in the mirror. Not too shabby, she thought to herself. Her friends fixed her hair into their identical updos and talked about the day to come. Aurora felt a sense of uneasiness inside her since she had never told any of them how she felt about Tristan.

She trusted them more than she wanted to admit but there was a mysterious tug in her heart telling her not to. "So, Aurora, tell us more about your little departure. It reminded me of your first disappearance." Roxy said with a glint of mischief in her gray eyes.

Aurora shuddered and thought of a good explanation. Now that she thought about it there was none. "I had a client requesting me to be back in FL nothing else," Aurora said coldly. Her friends stared as she looked away from them and they snickered in an unladylike manner. Aurora gazed at each of them sharply and opened her mouth to speak but was cut off by Jen.

"Sweetheart, we know it was because of Tristan. You could've just said it." She said as she twirled stray hair.

Aurora shook her head and faced them. "I had work too. Tristan was another reason, but not the main one. I have a life besides worrying about him." She said formally. Tina shook her head and reached out to hold Aurora's hand.

"How are you going to face him today? You two do have a history of running away from what you want." Alexa said as she eyed Aurora dramatically.

Aurora frowned deeper and shrugged. "What do you mean?" She said with a scowl. She didn't run away from anything. She went at everything at full speed. Didn't she?

"It's just that the both of you can't just get to the point about anything. You've been like this for more than years. Why not give it a break?" Tina said lightly.

"All I know is I'm going to set the record straight. I don't want to run away from it anymore and I don't think I ever have. Even if I do have feelings for him, I'm stubborn. I won't admit to loving him as much as I tend to. He hurt me once and I'm still getting over the first time around." she said with a blush creeping slowly onto her face. Her four friends giggled, and Aurora couldn't help but groan. This was why she didn't tell her feelings to people too much. Especially those love-struck ones who believed in fairy tale endings.

"Well, sweetheart you can't keep running from him. You don't know how long he's willing to hang around." Jen said nonchalantly.

Aurora soaked in the words and nodded. Now she had to think of a way to let it happen.

Chapter 27

Tristan was excited about the wedding. He had only been to one wedding when he was fourteen which he hadn't been able to remember well. He wasn't a romantic guy but the romantic air in a wedding was hard to resist. As he got ready with his friends, he listened as they talked about their love stories. They were sharing notes on their girlfriends or fiancés. He felt left out but still wanted to be filled in on their lives. Jack was as calm as he always was, but Tristan noticed a sense of distress in him. Jack tied his tie with shaky hands and tried to listen to Max talk about Renee, but Tristan knew his mind was elsewhere. Max had stopped talking and they were left in a comfortable silence.

"How are you feeling lover boy?" Tristan asked as he stared at Jack with a smile.

Jack smiled back and his eyes twitched with annoyance. "Good enough to realize I'm getting married in about two hours." He replied monotonously.

Tristan shook his head and pulled at his tie. "Listen homie, are you going to be the one to back out? Tina is the worrier, not you. Jen has texted me at least fifteen times telling me about how Tina keeps worrying her hair is too limp or her makeup is too much. I guess that comes with being a woman." Tristan said with a shrug.

Jack's face blanched and he sat in a chair with his head hung down. "I'm not going to back out. I love her Tristan, you know that. I wouldn't back out when I already promised her something. It's just hitting me now that I'm getting married. I feel so old." he said with a groan. Jack buried his face into his hands and his friends stared with big smiles plastered on their faces.

"Aw, how cute. The groom is acting like a blushing bride." Anthony said with a cheerful voice.

Jack looked up and eyed him spitefully. "Watch it Ant. You'll understand how I feel soon." He said with a harsh tone.

Anthony held his hands up in surrender, but a smile crept onto his face quickly. "Just relax man. Think about it. You're marrying the girl you love and have loved since your freshmen year in high school. Not all people marry the one they absolutely love." Tristan said with a small smile.

Jack's eyes brightened and he smirked. "What a Casanova thing to say. So cute." Jack said as he stood from his seat. He pulled his tuxedo jacket from its hanger and pulled it over his shoulders.

Tristan grinned widely and shook his head. "Yeah, if only I didn't have to clam up when Aurora talks to me," Tristan said with a mini groan. The boys looked at him with devilish grins and Tristan smacked his forehead.

"What is up with you two? It's always been like this, and you don't want to fix it? Neither of you don't deserve this chase. Especially Aurora. The poor girl is such an icy person now. She used to be so happy and fun-loving. She still is but she has that hesitation when she's happy as if she doesn't think she deserves it. I'm not blaming you for that, but you were a big part in that." Max said as he tied on his shoe.

Tristan pondered about that and heard a knock-on Anthony's room door. Anthony walked over and opened the door to display a wheezing Manny.

"Sorry. I'm. Late." he said with labored breaths. The men pulled him inside the room, and he plopped onto the bed unceremoniously.

"Why are you late man? This is my wedding day and I'm already freaking out!!" Jack said in a deathly whisper. Manny looked up at Jack and smiled.

"I went to go check on the girls. I have to admit all of them look hot." He said with an impish grin. Each of the men's heads turned at Manny and eyed him with dismal, dark looks. Manny smiled and sat up. "I only speak the truth. But don't worry. At the end of the day, I'm not the one going home with them. Well, maybe besides Aurora." Manny said as he shot his brother a sweet smile. Manny delved into his brother's look more and winked at him. Tristan tried all he could not to strangle his mother's baby, so he shot him a dirty look instead.

Anthony observed Tristan and grinned. "Calm down buddy. We all know you're going to Casanova here today. I mean, who can resist a little romance in a wedding?" Anthony said as he patted Tristan's on the back. Tristan rolled his eyes and stared out the window. He was ready for all of it. This was the biggest challenge in his life, and he decided to wing it.

Chapter 28

Everywhere was covered with flowers. Pink, purple, and white covered the tables and altar. Aurora sat in an open chair an hour and a half before the wedding and watched as everyone fussed over last-minute details. She looked at the front of the mini chapel and smiled faintly. The wedding wasn't exactly where she thought she would see Tristan again formally, but she decided to take it. Today was a day full of happy people and she decided she would have to function as such. Somehow, her mind wandered to her dream wedding. She wanted a beach wedding with Lilies. Hell, even the dress she was wearing at this moment was somewhat what she could see her bridesmaids wearing. Maybe she was overthinking it, but it was what she wanted. All she needed to make that wedding happen was the groom. But he didn't exist. Not even one bit.

She looked up at the blue sky. Miles away, the dark clouds invaded the next town. Aurora hoped the rain wouldn't take the wedding indoors. What better way to begin the deep relationship of their marriage than rain falling on their parade? Aurora grinned and shook her head as she laughed at the thought.

"You know, laughing to yourself is a sign of insanity?" she heard a voice rumble behind her. She smirked knowingly.

"Maybe you should wipe that smile off your face, darling. I can hear it in your voice." She said to the awaiting person behind her. She gazed up at their faces and felt her heart skip a beat.

"But you told me once you loved my smile. Tell me more lies why don't you dear?" he said gravely. She stood up and frowned deeply.

"Please. You were the one who said you loved me first and then you skipped out on me. And you call me the liar." Aurora snorted.

"Well, I thought things were working out for us last time you were here, but you skipped out on me. If that was your way of vengeance, I already used that. You just keep using the same tricks on me. I didn't do anything else so you can't either." Tristan said with a cold tone. Aurora raised her eyebrow and crossed her arms in front of her.

She heard footsteps behind her and turned to see Mike with a blanched face. "Sorry. I, uh never, um mind. See you later." He said as if he was a deer in headlights. He turned on his toes and scurried off. She groaned and slapped her forehead.

Tristan watched as Mike walked off tensely and looked back to Aurora. "He is quite the charmer. What do you see in him or is he just another plaything for your entertainment? I sure know how that feels." He grumbled.

Aurora stepped back in shock. "What do you mean?" she asked. He stepped toward her and glared unconsciously. "I thought things were working out for us, but it turns out you and Mike still have a thing. Do you ever stop and think about anything past this chase? Let me be more direct on how I feel?" He said as he shoved his hands in his pockets. She snorted and turned on her heel. She walked away from him slowly and looked up at the suddenly dark sky. Tristan walked to keep in step with her and she pulled her heels off. She walked on the grass without speaking to him. She stopped as they were far away from the wedding area and frowned at him, turning her body toward him fully. "Why do you care what goes on between Mike and me? Last I checked you were more than happy to let me out of your life! Why change it after so many years? Why now you moronic ignorant jackass?!?" She screamed as she pushed him off balance.

Tristan staggered backward onto the grass and stared at her with shock. She needed this closure. Her body shook from her anger, and she felt a weight be lifted from her soul. She felt the wet grass under her feet and tried to focus on the situation unfolding. She was being a total crazy bitch, but she needed to let this out. Holding it in any longer would have destroyed her more. Tristan sat on a dry patch of grass and looked down at his shoes. "Me?! What about you and being on that high horse you seem to think you're always on? It's always been about my faults, but you have part the blame. A relationship is made between two people making mistakes. Not just one. So, try to tell me about your part of the story. Do you know the one where you're always the good girl? I have a different more realistic version. I know I broke your heart, and I regret it more than you know, but don't you think we should just give it up already and realize what we both want?" Tristan fumed as he looked up at her.

She grunted and played with the frills on her dress. "This is so like you! Being a stubborn, ignorant guy!! Can't you wake up and act like it wasn't just about you!!" Aurora said icily.

He sighed and shook his head. He was mentally and physically tired of it. Aurora shook her head and shifted her weight. "I know I've made mistakes, but I need you to understand my point of view. My adult life has been focused on you and how badly you hurt me. Did you love me back then like you said you did? Don't you think I have a reason to be this mad? You decide to barge into my life again and pretend nothing went wrong. Give me a reason I can't be able to think the way I want to and believe what I want to believe." She shouted again, flailing her arms about, and losing her sanity.

Tristan stood up and looked into her eyes strongly. She had no idea how he felt. He tried to find the perfect words beside his thoughts but went with his thoughts anyway. It was now or never. "Because… It's because… I love you, Aurora. I always have, it's just that I was stupid enough to let you go. I'm tired of just running away from all of it. I know it took me years, but I just needed to see what would happen. I can't stop thinking about you. When I saw you again at your mom's house, I felt horrible. So many years can do a lot to someone, so I kept thinking everything through and every little detail of us. So, tell me now if you don't love me back, I don't think I'd be able to take it later. Tell me if you aren't willing to forgive and forget the past." He whispered.

She felt her body become numb and she bit her lip roughly to pull herself out of a daze. He loved her. She tried to believe it was real, but she was too insecure. She knew she was still at the tip of the edge of deciding if she loved him or not, but she was willing to stick around and wait. She needed to be around him. His existence was always on her mind. God, why was she so stubborn?? Here he was, in all his pride and glory, announcing his love for her and she was acting like a selfish bitch again. Their heated discussion caused her to realize it wasn't always supposed to be that way. They could talk like normal adults. She knew she couldn't run from it anymore. He was right. Running was always their action for things that involved happiness. Even if she wanted commitment, she was the one ruining her chances of it. Who cared if they were scared? It was time to run at full speed toward their fears and be full of adventure. Being scared for tomorrow was overrated when you still had to live today. She decided she was done with it all. It was now or never. "I don't know yet Tristan. If I say I can't feel anything, it's like I'm lying to myself, but I know I feel something. It's not exactly love yet, but I guess it could become it if you're willing to stick around." She said as she looked away from his wistful gaze.

He smiled at her quickly and pulled her off the ground. She shrieked with laughter and realized everything felt normal. It felt as if he was meant to be here with her. Carrying her and smiling with her. He twirled her around and her musical laughter filled his ears. He leaned in for a kiss and was rewarded with her participation in it. Warmth spread over her body and latched her arms around his neck for a closer touch. To him, it felt so right. It was just a kiss, but it was a milestone for them. It was the start of the end of their life. The closeness she wanted was found. She was happy. For once in her heartbreaking life, she was happy. Her heart was returned to her and both of their hearts were united. The one person to makes her happy is Tristan out of all of them. Everything was behind them and her only worry was that the moment would have ended.

Epilogue

"Mommy, look at this!!" a little boy said as he ran toward Aurora. He held a tiny car in his little chubby hand and waved it around. She bent over and looked at him with a smile. "That's cute, who's it from?" He giggled, his deep brown eyes glittering with happiness. "Daddy gave it to me!! Isn't it cool??" he said as he jumped up in down in the grass. She laughed and kissed him on his dark matted hair. "Yeah R.J., it is." She said as she scooped him up and carried him. They stayed out in the warm sunny weather, and she heard loud crying along with soothing hushing. Aurora looked up and saw Tristan holding their four-month-old baby, Faith. R.J. smiled wide and wiggled in his mother's arms. He ran loose and walked up to his dad. Tristan bent over and showed R.J. his little sister. R.J. placed a finger on her cheek, and she cooed lightly. Faith opened her eyes showing their bright blue luminescence. Aurora watched from afar and smiled. Her love for Tristan was growing every day. It had been six years since they had decided to bury the pain and restart everything.

Her dad had tried to make up with her and they had attempted to make things work. Her parents had both talked to each other after sixteen years. They talked things out and they learned to understand each other better. Tristan and she were married and now had two kids. Seeing Tristan in this scene made her feel as if it weren't real. To her, it was just a dream. He was just an amazing dream to her. But he wasn't, he was her reality and her happiness. Tristan walked toward her slowly and she felt her heart flutter. Tristan handed her Faith and Aurora held her baby close. R.J. opened his arms wide and begged his dad to carry him. Tristan smiled at this demand and hoisted the boy up. He leaned down to his wife and gave her a lingering kiss. He didn't know the events in their shaky lifestyle would end this way. It seemed so perfect. When R.J. was older, he would explain how he broke his mother's heart and how stupid his mistakes were. Even his little angel Faith would hear of the tale.

The sound of the young boy saying daddy, with his big brown eyes glimmering, made Aurora question everything. Now, standing face to face with it all made her understand the truth. This was how it was supposed to be. She tried to think she hadn't run away from things, but it was true, she had. In the end, running away was something important. It was from the things she never imagined could happen to her. That was why she ran. She was scared and didn't want things to turn out just as her parents' relationship had. She and Tristan were stubborn, and it was a crime worth so much. They took turns stealing each other's hearts but, in the end, they were meant to be for the other.

"STOP!! Daddy!!! Jill took my dolly!!" a shrill voice screamed. It was the reunion of an unusual group. It had been nearly a few years since Aurora and Tristan had gotten through the last hurdle and Jack and Tina were married. They had twin daughters, Jill, and Alice. They were both eight and at an obnoxious stage of their lives. Jack was worried boys, like him at one point, would have made moves on his daughters. Tina had told him that he didn't have to worry about that till they reached eleven, but he had sworn it was starting now. Roxy and Anthony have had two boys so far. Their names were Junior and Harry. Nothing like their parents Junior was seven and Harry was six. They had been exact copies of their father and Aurora knew they were going to break hearts. Max and Renee were engaged and happier than ever. Jen had found a suitable man for her and oddly enough Mike was that man. "Okay, give it back to her Jill," Jack said in a fatherly tone.

Aurora couldn't help but giggle as she heard this, and Jack gave her a cold glare as she pulled the girls away from each other. "Not helping Aur." he said with a groan. She smiled and carried Jill on her shoulder. "Don't take your sister's doll Auntie Aurora will buy you one, but you have to promise you won't take Alice's doll. Understand?" Aurora said with a grin. The little girl smiled widely and nodded. She let the girl down and she ran away to her mom.

"Wasn't that nice? At least now they're going to get spoiled by you. Tina and I aren't losing money." Jack said with a grin.

R.J. walked up to her and frowned visibly. In his hand, a half-eaten lollipop stood proudly and was the obvious cause of the young boy's distress. "M-my l-lolli-lollipo-p, Daddy ate it," he said as tears started to fall. Aurora pulled the boy toward her and her friends laughed.

"Aww…love. Daddy's a bully. Uncle Jack over there will buy you a ton of them don't worry now don't cry." she said as she held the boy against her. The young boy sniffled lightly and nodded dejectedly. He ran off and all the children left the room slowly.

"So Aur, where is your bully of a husband?" Anthony asked with a grin. She sighed and blushed lightly. Even if it had been quite a while, the word husband sounded so foreign to her.

"Talking behind my back now? Won't you ever grow up Anthony?" Tristan said as he walked in. Ant shook his head and brought his drink to his lips.

"Live a little Tristan don't be so serious life's too short." He said as Tristan walked to Aurora.

He sat next to her unceremoniously and she climbed onto his lap. His arm snaked its way across her waist, and he held her tightly. Aurora turned and looked at him wistfully. "R.J. came here crying because you ate his lollipop." She said as he nuzzled her shoulder.

"I'll buy him another one?" he said against her shoulder. She smiled and slapped him lightly.

"You made my baby cry!" she said harshly. Tristan adjusted her on his lap, and she wrapped her arms around him tightly.

"I'm getting the feeling that now that I'm a dad it's my fault if something like that happens." He said as he gave her a small smile.

Aurora shook her head and heard heavy footsteps hurry into the room. "Mommy... mommy!! I think I'm in love!!" Alice said as she ran to Tina. Aurora felt Tristan laugh at her and she heard the others laugh along.

Jack shook his head and groaned loudly. "Sweetie don't do this to daddy. You fall in love when you're in high school or college or when you turn fifty, not at eight." He growled lightly.

Tina laughed and held the young girl close. "With whom honey?" She asked with a smile.

Alice jumped up and down and smiled wide. "With Junior!! He likes apples, the color blue, and sunsets and he loves me back!!! We like the same things!!" the young girl screamed.

Jack gave Ant a hostile look and pulled his little girl away from her mother. "Love later for now just be a little girl," Jack said as the girl walked away. The room burst into laughter and Aurora smiled widely.

"Overprotective daddy," Anthony said with a devilish grin. Aurora grinned and realized everything was going to repeat itself. This was her life just as she always wanted. The laughter and smiles grew with each day. Their hearts were at peace and their only worries were whether tomorrow would be as amazing as this exact moment.